DATE DUE

	JE 5 07		
JA 28 '94			
MY 27 '94			
AG 4 '94			
NO 28 '94			
DE 23 '94			
MY 19 '95			
ND 27 '95			
MR 22 '96			
DE 11 '96			
AP 11 '97			
MY 11 '98			
DE 18 '98			
DE 18 '99			
DE 8 00			
DE 18 '03			
DE 12 05			
MR 23			

My Life on the Street

My Life on the Street

Memoirs Of A Faceless Man

by

Joe Homeless

NEW HORIZON PRESS
Far Hills, New Jersey

Library of Congress Catalog Card Number: 91-67990

Joe Homeless
  MY LIFE ON THE STREET

ISBN 0-88282-102-4
New Horizon Press

1997 1996 1995 1994 1992 / 5 4 3 2 1

Manufactured in the United States of America

Full many a gem of purest ray serene,
The dark unfathomed caves of ocean bear,
Full many a flower is born to blush unseen,
And waste its sweetness on the desert air.

—Thomas Gray
  "Elegy Written in a Country Churchyard"

Acknowledgements

The book that you are about to read was a great personal achievement for me, considering the fact that I can't spell or type and know zero about English.

The book is also a tribute to the humanity of all the people who helped me see the project through: the thirty-five people who took time out of their lives to type my book from raw tapes and scribbled-over partial manuscripts; the people who could not do any typing but who instead gave me whatever change they had in their pockets so I could buy good food and vitamins; and the doctors, lawyers and others who gave me the benefit of their knowledge for free.

These are the people who made it possible for a bum to walk with giants.

Society being what it is, many of the people that helped me do this book and survive these twelve-plus years living on the street chose not to be mentioned because it could cause them personal difficulties. That is why there is no list of names on this acknowledgement page. I did not want to have just a partial list, so there is no list.

After you read my book, I would like you to do me three favors, whether you think I am a genius or a jerk.

(1) Say a prayer for every homeless person that you see;

(2) If you have any spare change in your pocket, give it to them; and

(3) Send a letter to the Mayor, Governor and President to ask them to back off on the plan to drive the homeless off the streets, out of the mass transit system and bus stations and into the shelters, where the most inhuman living conditions exist.

I would like you to keep in mind that most of the homeless are homeless not because they are drug addicts, alcoholics or mentally incompetent. They are in the street as a result of the sick economy. The politicians who fouled up the economy think it is a good idea to put the homeless where they can't be seen so no one will ask them why so many people are living in the streets and subways, begging money to survive. I ask you to help their voices be heard.

Joe Homeless

Contents

Preface

"This life, you might say, is the American version of the German-Japanese death marches of World War II. The Japanese would take the American prisoners, while the Germans would take Jews, and they'd force them into a death march. That's exactly what happens to the homeless when they're forced and herded, constantly on their feet, with no food or water."

"Or, you might say it's like the crucifixion of Christ. But the homeless do not carry a cross; they carry a shopping bag. And they're tormented and tortured every step of the way. Most homeless people don't live too long. The true numbers the media reports are not what you see on the street, or in the shelters—they are in Potter's Field, in the graveyard."

—Joe
(the homeless man)

Author's Note

These are my actual experiences, in my own words. I have tried to safeguard privacy by changing some names and, in some cases, I changed physical descriptions of people and the order of how things happened. Events involving the characters happened as described; only minor details have been changed.

1
The Talking Animal

---

*T*his is Homeless, the talking animal. This is the story of how I become homeless and what it is like to be a homeless person. The things you are about to read are all true and have consumed my life for about eleven years. I am not a drug addict, alcoholic, or convict and I wasn't a mental patient when this all started.

I was a hard-working guy, a guy with a trade most of my life, a high school graduate who finished in the upper half of his class. From age eighteen I had always made a decent living. In the last few years I was a mechanical contractor, repairing big appliances for restaurants, stores, and delis.

I had worked steadily, almost until the time I became one of the City's homeless. Having earned a certificate from the General Motors Mechanic's course, I began a small business fixing restaurant equipment. For a while it prospered, I bought a van, and I was working five or six jobs at the same time. I always had money to buy food and pay my rent. I trusted those who hired me and would only ask them to put ten percent down, until I completed their job.

Then I got hurt and could not work. Unfortunately, because of over-extension and no credit, I found myself with no cash. I had no money or health insurance. To be facing eviction and to have the landlord knocking at my door, looking for rent, was a new experience for me.

The apartment owners of the building I lived in were threatening me by this time. I had done nothing wrong, and certainly nothing that I could ever be ashamed of admitting to anybody.

Both my parents and I had lived in this four-room apartment on 120th Street in Manhattan for over twenty years. The apartment was rent-controlled and my rent was really low. That's the main reason I kept on living there after my parents passed away.

* * *

My story begins after I had turned thirty, in October 1979, when I received a Dispossess Notice from the landlord for non-payment of rent. It is formally called a Petition of Dispossess. What I should have done was go to court and get a court date, but since I didn't have the money to pay the rent, I thought it was pointless. Also, I knew there would not be any serious problem until I received a seventy-two hour notice. That notice gives you seventy-two hours to come up with the rent or the marshal will come knocking on your door to forcibly evict you.

I decided to wait until I got my seventy-two hour notice before I put any of my emergency plans into action. I had thought out my plan, which was to call my family and ask for some financial help for the first time in my life. And if they refused to help me, I would try welfare.

I kept on thinking, "There's got to be a way I can come up with some money to pay my rent and Con Edison, to get my lights turned back on, get myself out of this jam I'm in."

I didn't want to bother my family, which is quite large, until I got my seventy-two hour notice. I was proud and thought I could figure my own way out of this mess. Once I got the seventy-two hour notice, I would have no choice—then I would have to come up with the money right away.

I felt sure my family would help me. Many of them have their own private houses, and you might say they are upper middle-class people. After all, we

3

are Italians, and Italians are supposed to take care of their own. My family would have no reason not to help me out. But I had to prepare myself: if my family wouldn't help me, and if I got nowhere with welfare, then I would end up going into the street. What would I do then?

Now, as a mechanic I had a large assortment of tools, some of which I had bought, and some of which I had inherited from my father, who was a cabinet maker. There were far too many, and some were too heavy to actually take with me. If I were evicted I could only take the most valuable tools I had, the ones most difficult to replace. I would take some electronic test equipment which I had made myself, and some that I had bought, two telephone answering machines that were almost new, and a few light hand tools, which I might need to make a living somewhere else.

Upset, I started to look around the apartment. I remembered there was a special, fat leather pouch that my father used to have. It was about the size of a school bag, with a zipper around it. He had lots of important papers in it, even letters he had received before I was born. After my mother and father died, I put their death certificates in there too. There was a deed to the family plot where both of my parents were buried, and all sorts of correspondence that I never seemed to find the time to read through. I figured I'd better get into these documents now to find out what was valuable, what I should take with me and what I could leave behind.

4

Sifting through the box, I found a whole load of old photographs: pictures—turned sepia and cream by time—of my father, my mother, their parents, all sorts of cousins, aunts, photographs of me when I was growing up, and children in the family who now were adults. I started to read some of the correspondence, and I began to learn things that I never knew before about my family.

There were some letters from my Aunt Mildred to my father that said she wouldn't pay for the funeral or for the headstone for my uncle's grave. Aunt Mildred was talking about my Uncle Dominique, who we used to call, "Uncle Bim." I remembered him from when I was a kid.

When I was maybe four- or five-years old, my father and I used to go over to Uncle Dominique's house and my father would give him a couple of bucks to buy food or just to make life a little easier for him. I can remember my Uncle Dominique's dog was named Mitsi.

Uncle Dominque lived in a three-room ground floor apartment with a bathtub in the kitchen. All the time that I was there, when I was a kid, I never saw him turn on the lights. I don't know whether he had electricity or not. He had some kind of trade, but I don't know exactly what it was. I know he was very old, and he had no wife or children. That much I remember. I know that he was sick, but I don't know what was wrong with him.

I was curious about how my Uncle Dominique died. What kind of disease did he have? Could it be hereditary?

I found a letter from our family doctor, his name was Doctor Zee. The upper corner of this letter listed Dr. Zee's office hours, which were six days a week plus half a day on Sunday. The letter said that my Uncle Dominique should be admitted to the hospital. He had to be "worked up." But the letter didn't say what was wrong.

Doctor Zee was the same doctor who had delivered me. He was my father's friend, they grew up together in the same neighborhood. And from the stories my father used to tell me about Doctor Zee, he wasn't what you would call the average kind of person. When he was a kid and people in the neighborhood used to find a dog, cat, or any animal that was hit by a car or a trolley car, they used to take the injured animals to him. He was only like fifteen- or sixteen-years old, and he used to operate on dogs, cats, horses—you name it, he used to do it. And he cured many of these animals. He was really what you would call a healer.

My father always talked highly of him, and I can remember how well he treated me everytime I went to his office, when I was a little kid. He always used to give me a little piece of candy, a lollypop, chewing gum, or some empty rolls of his adhesive tape.

And I remember how my mother used to pay Dr. Zee. Well, you never had to pay him directly. He used to have a basket in his outer office and after he treated you or saw you, you would just throw money in the basket, whatever you could afford. And if you had no money, that was okay, too. If you were sick, you would go see him, and he would help you. He made house calls seven days a week, twenty-four hours a day.

I wonder what the doctors of today would think about Doctor Zee? The doctors of today, they've got computerized billing systems. I wonder how Doctor Zee could live on just what people would give him or what they could afford?

But he made a fairly good living, because I remember my father always used to joke with him about why he always drove a La Salle (an expensive car). Dad said it was because they were good getaway cars and Dr. Zee was a crook (charged too much). Doctor Zee always used to laugh and say, "Yeah, you're right." He and my father were very, very, good friends.

La Salles were the same cars crooks used when they would pull bank robberies in the old gangster movies. If you've ever seen the movie, *The Roaring Twenties*, the big black cars they used were La Salles. La Salle eventually became Cadillac.

I remember the Sunday when Doctor Zee died. One of his patients took ill and they called Dr. Zee. He went to see the sick man, even though it was Sunday. After examining him, Dr. Zee felt that the patient should get to the hospital immediately. He didn't want to wait for an ambulance, so Dr. Zee tried to carry the patient down to his car. The sick man lived on the fifth floor of a walk-up. Doctor Zee had a heart attack and died while he was carrying him downstairs.

I found more correspondence from people who knew Doctor Zee, and in them were acclamations of what a wonderful guy they all thought he was. He was certainly a far cry from most of the doctors I know today.

Well, by reading the correspondence I found out that my Uncle Dominique had made Aunt Mildred the beneficiary of his insurance policy. After he died, Aunt Mildred got whatever money he had. Exactly how much I don't know.

My father thought that since Aunt Mildred was the beneficiary of the insurance, she should be the one to pay for Uncle Dominique's funeral. But she didn't think so, and wanted the city to bury Uncle Dominique. Aunt Mildred thought it was more important to take the insurance money and buy a house in New Jersey. My father was the one who finally paid for the headstone on his grave. After this dispute, I remember that for many years my father and Aunt Mildred would not talk.

* * *

I started to think, "Gee, when it comes to money, some of my family are pretty tight." Well, Aunt Mildred was only one member of my family. I didn't figure that the whole family was like that.

Flipping through the papers in the box, I came on a photograph of my Aunt Loulou. I remembered being in her house one time and noticing that she had four boxes of pasta on the kitchen table. I asked her, "What are you going to do with all that pasta?"

She said, "I'm going to send it to my husband." (This was my Uncle Mike, who got deported to Italy for being an undesirable alien.)

I asked my aunt, "Why are you going to send him pasta? If he's living in Italy he's got pasta; that's the one thing Italy's got plenty of."

She said, "Well, it's not that I want to send him pasta, 'cause I want to send him cigarettes."

She would take the pasta out of the boxes and put packages of cigarettes in them and then put some pasta on top of the cigarettes. Then she would very carefully glue the boxes back together again so they could get through Customs, because cigarettes were difficult to get in Italy or expensive, I don't know exactly what.

Thinking of my Aunt Loulou, who I always thought was a little bit off the wall, made me start to laugh. Then my dog "C.T." started to grab my feet.

9

He thought I wanted to play. As I pushed him away I kept wondering, what am I going to do with C.T. if I wind up on the street?

That started me thinking how I had found my dog on a winter morning. When my father had his stroke and was in a coma for over a year, I used to go to the hospital and stay throughout the night with him because he was very sick and might die at any time. If he woke up out of his coma and asked for me, I wanted to be there.

One cold, snowy, January morning about 6 a.m., I was coming home from visiting my dad and came upon a dog in my hallway, curled up next to the steam heater. He was so skinny, you could see the ribs sticking out of his body. There were scabs and welts on his back. He looked like he had been beaten and mistreated.

I walked over to the dog and looked at him and he looked at me, and I think we must have made a mind link. His eyes fastened on me and he jumped to his feet, with his tail between his legs and his ears down, because he was scared. Nevertheless, he followed me up the stairs to my apartment. I could hear his paws thumping on the tile steps. Later, I found out that his claws were either worn off or never grew.

I didn't want to get involved with another dog. The dog I had when I was growing up had died a few years before. Losing that dog had really hurt me too much to think of going through that again with another dog. Still, this dog looked so forlorn that I thought I'd bring him some food, maybe some milk and water, and put it near the steam heater so he could eat. This puppy was cuddly and small, somebody was bound to adopt him. I brought him some chopped meat and went back to my apartment.

An hour or two passed and I heard him sniffing and searching. Then I made a mistake. I opened the door. He came in and that was it. I tried to get rid of him many times, to give him away to people, but could never find anybody who wanted to take him that I trusted; so I wound up keeping him.

I kept thinking about my friendship with C.T. and how important he was to me. He always used to be able to get me out of a bad or solemn mood. Any time I had problems in my life his playfulness always managed to cheer me up.

Right after my parents died, I was painting my apartment and was in a sad mood thinking about them. C.T. nestled up to me trying to console me. But I kept tripping over him, so I poked him with the paint brush and told him to stop getting in my way. Then he grabbed the paint brush in his mouth and by the time I got it back from him, he had put wide blue stripes all over the floor and chewed up the handle too badly to use. I had to go out to the store and get a new paint brush.

When I left, I didn't put the top on the can of paint tightly, and for some reason my dog thought water-based blue paint was delicious. I was gone a few hours. When I came back to the house, I saw the paint can lying open. C.T.'s nose and tongue were coated blue. He had drunk up most of the paint.

Frightened, I thought he was going to die. So I immediately brought him to the Dog and Cat Hospital with the can of paint, so that the doctor could read the ingredients in the paint.

An old, gangly doctor examined my dog and then said, "Well, uh, how much paint did he drink?"

I said, "I don't know, there was only a little bit left."

He said, "Well, he's acting fine, I'll give him a few blood tests, but I think he'll be okay. Bring him home, and if any symptoms develop, bring him back."

I brought C.T. back to the apartment and tried to clean up some of the blue paw prints and stripes. Then I scolded him, even though it was really my fault. I should have closed the can of paint better. But how could I know my dog liked blue paint?

Well, C.T. suffered no ill effects from eating this blue paint and he did manage to give me a few laughs. When I brought him outside so he could do his duty and he moved his bowels, it was blue. It looked like he was making little birthday cake decorations. I thought that was pretty funny and I joked around with the boss of an Italian bakery in the neighborhood.

I said, "Hey, you want my dog, he's good for making decorations on birthday cakes."

He also thought it was funny and we stood there belly-laughing together. As always, my dog was successful in making me feel better.

C.T. nestled up to me now. I wondered if I was going to be as lucky as my dog. If I became homeless, would I find somebody to take care of me?

I kept racking my brain, trying to figure out how was I supposed to come up with money for the rent and Con Ed. Nothing came to me, finally I decided to get my mind off it for a while. Maybe something would come to me later. I tried my great escape, baseball.

I had always wanted to become a baseball player for as long as I could remember and I received one offer to play some semi-pro baseball in Florida. I had planned on taking it up as soon as I graduated from high school. Then my father had a heart attack a few months before I graduated and my mother told me, "No, you can't go play baseball, you have to stay home and take care of your father."

So I had to forget the baseball career, go to work and help support my family, and take care of my father. It was really the wrong decision, 'cause as it worked out I could do very little to help my father, it was all up to the doctors and hospitals, not me.

All that seemed to have happened a long time

ago, now it was October 1979—World Series time. I always listened to the games on my small, battery-powered, portable radio. And I started to think about past World Series games.

I thought about all the dramatic moments in World Series history, such as when Cookie Lavagetto broke up the Bill Bevans "no-hitter" in the bottom of the ninth inning. I remembered when Don Larson pitched his no-hit perfect game in the World Series, and how Yogi Berra jumped in his arms and hugged him.

I began wondering whether this World Series was going to be as exciting as the World Series of the past. This time it wasn't going to be a Yankee World Series, and for me that was a letdown, because I had been a Yankee fan for my whole life.

But this World Series might be remembered for the time when two of the finest third basemen that had ever played clashed and tried to see who could outdo the other. First, there was Mike Schmidt of The Philadelphia Phillies. I believe Mike led the National League in home runs. And he was a Gold Glove fielder, always a power hitter and a threat at the plate. Second, was George Brett of the Kansas City Royals. George almost hit 400 that year and was considered on of the finest hitters in baseball.

I was wondering, "What's going to be remembered for this game, what dramatic moments?"

I started to listen to the game and then they kept talking about how George Brett was having physical problems. They didn't know whether he would be able to play in all of the World Series games. Unfortunately, George was ill and might not be starting. Naturally, reporters had to find out what was wrong with him.

George turned out to have inflamed hemorrhoids and he had to have emergency surgery. For the first time in history, Preparation-H bought network TV advertising time during a World Series. This made me laugh. Boy, all the sports historians looking back at this World Series probably wouldn't be talking about great plays, great hitting, or great pitching. They would probably remember this time as the George Brett Butt World Series.

While listening, I found an old shopping cart in the apartment. I began putting in it things that I would need in case I did get evicted—some of my electronic tools and electrical test equipment, two telephone answering machines with remote controls, a few light hand tools, and my father's leather pouch with the important papers in it. To this I added my birth certificate, the deed to the family cemetery plot, and some photos and letters I wanted to save.

Afterwards, I started to ponder my fate and began to wonder what I was going to do. What move could I make? It was Sunday night. I knew the courts and the post office were going to be open on Monday, and also it would be the seventh and final game of the World Series. Would I get my seventy-two hour notice on Monday. Maybe somebody would foul up, forgot all about me and I could at least watch the Series end.

Jittery and unsure of the future, I lay in bed but could only sleep fitfully.

2
Knocking On Every Door

When I got up Monday morning, I was very troubled and depressed. I knew I was going nowhere, and going nowhere in a hurry. And I couldn't figure out how I could come up with any money.

Then, at about 10 a.m., I heard a knock on the door. I disregarded it. A loud voice called me by name and someone knocked so hard this time, that it almost knocked the door off its hinges. I opened the door and saw the superintendent and a marshal. About fifteen or twenty people from the neighborhood stood behind them.

The marshal, a crusty-looking old man, said, "You're going to have to leave this apartment. The landlord has taken possession."

I asked, "What do ya mean, I'm going to have to leave my apartment? I never got a seventy-two hour notice, and you can't evict somebody unless you give them a seventy-two hour notice."

He said, "Look, a seventy-two hour notice was sent—and you're claiming you didn't receive it, well, go get a lawyer and go to court. Now either you leave or I'll call the cops and have them forcibly put you out of your apartment."

I said, "Look, I can't leave. I never got the seventy-two hour notice, that is *illegal*." (This is how many homeless become homeless illegally.)

He said, "Well, it was sent. If you got any problems, go down to the Landlord and Tenants Court and tell it to a judge, but you're going to leave. You're going to leave with the cops or without the cops, and we're going to confiscate all your tools for safekeeping until after you vacate."

I said, "You can't evict me and you can't take my tools. You cannot take a mechanic's tools and end his ability to make a living."

The marshal said, "Look, nobody's going to steal your tools. The super is going to put them down in the basement in a special room and lock it. Any time you want them, you come back and you can have them, nobody's going to touch them."

But I insisted and finally he partially relented

and let me have some of the tools. The rest he stored in the basement.

I said, "Give me some time, I got to get some of my stuff together that I wanna take with me."

He replied, "Alright, you got five, ten minutes," —then he turned away.

I went back into my apartment, packed everything else I could in the shopping cart, and put on heavy clothing. I knew it would be getting cold soon. I tried to look around the apartment to see if I had forgotten anything that might be of value or importance. I don't know how long I spent looking around, but the marshal wouldn't wait any longer. He and the super pushed the door open and announced, "You're going to have to leave right now." The super was drinking a can of beer and threw it on the floor. The beer splashed in every direction as he started to change the lock on the door.

I glared at the super, "Hey, this is my house, you don't do that shit in my house." Angrily I went on, "You pick it up or I'm going to clean the beer up with you."

The super stared at me, picked up the beer can, and began to clean the spilt beer with a rag he had in his back pocket. All sorts of people from the neighborhood stood peering at us from the hallway, like this was an event.

Then the marshal said to me, "Do you want us to call the ASPCA for your dog?"

I shook my head, "No, because the ASPCA will

19

just destroy him because he is old and nobody will adopt him. I'll take C.T. with me."

Then he said, "Well, you gotta go now." So I left, thinking I'd sell some of the valuable stuff that I had to a few people I knew, raise some money, and get hold of a lawyer to see if I could get my apartment back. I knew I couldn't possibly raise enough money to pay my back rent and Con Edison. But maybe the lawyer could think of something. "Just let me get some money," I thought, "that would be the first move."

I had an acquaintance who was a carpenter/ contractor in the Bronx. I decided to try him first, because he always used to like my telephone answering machine and the one he had was always broken. I figured I could sell him mine, which was much better than his and raise some money. I walked down First Avenue toward the First Avenue Bridge, walked over it to the Bronx, and went to see my friend Vee, the carpenter/contractor.

I was lucky, he hadn't gone out with his men on a job yet. He said, "Hey Joe, what happened to you?"

I says, "Things are bad right now, I need some money."

He says, "Well, uh. . . ."

We started talking and I said, "Well, look, I got two telephone answering machines, they are worth a bundle; what will you offer me?"

He said, "Well, let me see the machines."

I showed him the machines, and he says, "Are these legit?"

I said, "Yes they're legit, I even got the bills."

He said, "Look, I'll give you a hundred bucks for both machines."

I said, "Are you crazy? A hundred bucks? They're worth a lot more than that."

He replied, "A hundred bucks is better than nothing."

He was right; so I took the hundred. He asked, "What are you going to do with all those assorted tools and things you got?"

I said, "I don't know, why?"

He said, "Cause I'll give you an extra fifty bucks for everything."

I said, "Forget that, you know they're worth a whole lot more money than that, that's my living and this is how I'm going to eat when I get another apartment."

He said, "Look, I'll hold them for you, nobody's going to bother them."

I said, "I know you better than that; you think you know how to use some of this stuff and you're going to end up breaking it."

He said, "No, no, I won't break any of it, I know how to use these tools."

I says, "Yeah, sure you're a carpenter, you do carpentry work, electronic equipment you don't know anything about." I left Vee's shop with the hundred bucks, my dog, and the shopping cart.

As I was walking, one of the wheels broke on

the shopping cart. Now I only had three wheels and the cart was pretty heavy because of the load I was carrying. I knew I couldn't drag this stuff around much further in a broken shopping cart. I thought of an acquaintance who owned a grocery store around 138th Street in the Bronx, right on Willis Avenue. He used to like me. I had fixed some equipment he had that another mechanic had given up on. Maybe he could keep my tools and dog.

I went over there. He looked surprised to see me, "Hey Joe, what happened to you?"

I answered, "That's a long story. Right now I'm in a little trouble; do you think you could do me a favor? Could you hold some of my tools and my dog for me until I can come back and get them?"

He kind of chewed on his lip, "Well, I can't keep your dog 'cause I got a lot of dogs already and they'd start fighting, I got enough headaches without having to break up a bunch of dogs. But I'll be more than happy to hold your tools for you."

I felt apprehensive, "Now these tools are valuable to me. If you lose these tools, I won't be able to make a living."

He looked me straight in the eyes and said, "Don't worry, I'll protect these tools with my life, nobody is going to touch them, I give you my word."

About a year later, I found out that his word wasn't worth much. When I got out of the hospital, I went over to his place to ask him for my tools—

shrugging, he told me he didn't know what happened to them. But I asked around the neighborhood and found out he had sold them.

I left his store without my tools, but with my dog, the important papers, and the money I had from Vee, desperately thinking, "What am I going to do now? It's getting late; where am I going to spend the night?"

Almost all of my family had moved far away. The only one in my family who lived close to me was my Cousin Jill. Jill used to babysit me. She always spoke of how she had changed my diapers when I was a baby. I thought I would try her. She used to offer me food and ask me to stay overnight and said she worried about me. She told me that anytime I was in the neighborhood, I should go right up to her house and there would always be something to eat. I didn't think about the fact that she used to tell me that when she knew I was working and had a sports car and money in my pocket.

I thought, "There should be no reason why she wouldn't help me. I never had any real arguments with her or asked her for anything before." I thought she was soft-hearted, because I used to always see her cry at sad movies on television when I was a young boy. I didn't want to go up there begging, because it meant I was a failure. But with no real money and no prospects, I had no choice. I needed help, I needed a place to stay. The hundred bucks I had wouldn't last long if I tried to stay in a hotel. I would be broke in no time. I figured Cousin Jill would let me stay a couple of days in her big apartment. Maybe she could keep my dog for me, because her cat had died. Feeling better, I decided to go there.

Cousin Jill lived near 187th Street and Hoffman Avenue in the Bronx, where all the Italian delicatessens and grocery stores are. It's known as Little Italy. There would be a lot of good food up there. Slowly, I walked in that direction. My dog followed. I was taking my time getting there, because it was hard to get up the courage to ask for her help, but yet I knew I had to do it.

Feeling miserable, I trudged up Willis Avenue and then I got onto Third Avenue. Around 160th Street I started to encounter some gangs. Neighborhood people kept staring at me and following me down the street. First, they did nothing, then they started throwing things at me, like bottles, cans, all kinds of objects. I couldn't figure why these people were doing this.

I thought maybe it was because I was in a black neighborhood, or that my appearance was shabby, because the landlord had shut off the water in my apartment. But I didn't think I really looked that bad. So I started to walk a little bit faster. I knew once I got to 187th Street near Arthur Avenue, no black gangs would go in that neighborhood, because it was Italian. And since I'm Italian, I thought that should protect me.

I got to Jill's building about 8 p.m., but I couldn't get in. The building had private doors that were locked and there was no bell on the outside that I could ring. I found a public phone and called Jill's number. The phone rang about ten times. There was no answer. I figured, "Well let me wait around for a while, maybe she's in the building talking to one of her neighbors or maybe she went out to buy something."

I stood near the phone and thought hard about my Cousin Jill, wondering whether she had any feelings for me. I knew she would be financially able to help me, because her husband always used to drive around in Cadillacs; he made a good living.

As I stood there, people started to gather around me, staring. I certainly wasn't doing anything wrong. I tried again to call Jill. This time I got her on the phone. She recognized my voice; she said, "Oh yeah, how ya been?"

I said, "Not so good." I told her about the problems I was having. How I just got evicted from my apartment; how I didn't have any place to go, or much money. I asked if she could put me up for a few days, maybe give me some food, take care of my dog, hold some of my important papers.

In an annoyed voice she replied, "I can't do anything for you."

I said, "You always used to offer me invitations to come up there and have something to eat."

She answered, "Well it's different now. I heard

from people in your neighborhood that you're a bum and you were evicted out of your apartment."

I said, "Yeah, I just told you I'm having some bad times, I'd like to explain to you what the whole story is."

She cut me off, "Look, I don't want to hear what the whole story is; I really just don't want to be bothered."

I said, "Well, could you just hold some of my important papers for me? It isn't safe to drag them around with me."

She said, "I don't even want to see you."

I said, "You won't even hold my dog?"

She said, "No, my cat will wind up attacking him."

I sighed, "Your cat died."

She said, "No you're mistaken, my cat is still alive." Then she said, "Look, please, I don't want to be bothered. Don't call me again," and she hung up.

Slowly, I replaced the receiver and started to leave. Then I realized I had nowhere to go. She had no reason to turn her back on me. I wondered why she had. Then I started to rationalize why she wouldn't help me. I kept thinking of the things that Aunt Lilli had told me after my mother died. Aunt Lilli and Cousin Jill were always very friendly.

I started to think back and remember what happened to my mother. After my father had died in August, 1968 my mother took ill. Not sick enough to go into the hospital, but ill. She kept it to herself. Then one night, in November of the same year, I was sitting down reading a book and she went out. She came back with some groceries, carefully put them in the refrigerator and turned to me, "Joe, please take me to the hospital."

Startled I asked, "Why, what's wrong?"

She said, "Well, I don't feel good. I haven't felt good for a while but I didn't want to go to the doctors when your father was so sick in the hospital. But I think I should go to the hospital now because something is really wrong."

I said, "Okay, Mom, what hospital do you want to go to?"

She told me.

I said, "Wait here." I went downstairs, got my car and moved it in front of the building, and went upstairs. I helped her down the stairs to my car and I took her to the hospital's emergency room.

She spoke to the nurse, then the nurse took my mother to one of the treatment rooms. I waited outside to see what the doctors had to say about my mother. I knew that my mother always had problems with hernias and her digestion. She'd had a few operations. Maybe something was acting up because of one of her earlier operations. Recently she had picked up a 'flu that was going around. Although she was coughing and sneezing, she never said anything else was wrong with her.

I was really worried, because I knew that when somebody loses a loved one, they may not want to live without them. Sometimes, their immune system breaks down and they fall prey to any disease that is around. Thinking about it, I realized that my mother really had let herself go since my father had died. It was the first time I actually knew that my mother's hair was naturally grey, 'cause my mother made her living as a beautician and she always did a beautiful job dyeing her hair. Now she looked old and unkempt. I waited and waited for the doctors to come.

Finally, a balding, mid-fiftyish doctor walked over. "Look, we are going to have to operate on your mother. She has serious gastro-intestinal problems, but she is far too run down to operate on immediately. We do have to go in as soon as we can. She probably hasn't been eating well for a long time and she's got that flu that has been going around.

"We're going to have to work her up very carefully, but we definitely have to go in surgically to correct her problems. First, we have to build her up and get her as strong as we can. We will give her some blood transfusions and an I.V. We're not going to go into her tonight. Maybe tomorrow, maybe the next day, we'll see how things go."

I asked, "Should I hang around; does she want to see me?"

He replied, "Well, we're going to sedate her, it's pointless for you to hang around. Come tomorrow. She'll be in her room. She should be able to talk and see you then. Try and tell the members of the family not to come and visit her for the next couple of days, because she'll be groggy and we may need to go in and operate on her really quick."

I replied, "Alright." He told me when visiting hours started the next day.

I went home. The next morning I went to the hospital to see my mother. She was heavily sedated. I saw the doctor who had first talked to me and asked, "Hey, what's going on?"

He seemed grim, "I'm going to have to operate on her now, I have no other choice. But she is very weak."

I said, "Is there anything else that you can do?"

He said, "No, the operation is the only thing that is going to help her."

I took a deep breath and gave my consent.

It was ten o'clock when they started to prep her for the operation (she had to wait because there were others before her who were more critically ill). I waited around till about seven or eight o'clock that night before they finally took her to the operating room. I went upstairs to the recovery room and spent the night drinking coffee.

Finally, around six or seven o'clock the next morning the doctor told me, "We've finished, she's very weak, but she is going to be okay."

Relieved, I thanked him and asked, "When is she going to be out of the anesthesia?"

He answered slowly, "Well, she won't be conscious for quite a while. Go home, come back later on today. She may be out of the anesthesia, she may not."

29

I nodded in reply.

Outside of the hospital, I got into my car and turned the ignition on, but the motor began to cough and sputter. I thought, "What a time for my car to be acting up."

I had a sports car with a special ignition system, something called dual points, to get optimum performance. There were only a few places that could service this car. I managed to drive to New Jersey to a place they call Gasoline Alley, where they handle all types of sports cars. They fixed the car while I waited impatiently.

Finally, I was able to get back to my apartment about 11 a.m. and feed my dog. While C.T. was eating, I called the hospital to see how my mother was doing. They said she was fine, resting comfortably. After my dog ate I took him outside. Then I went back to the apartment, drank some milk, ate a piece of toast, and went to bed. I was so tired I went out like a light.

Suddenly, my dog started barking at the door. People were noisily walking up and down the steps in the hallway. It woke me up. Peering outside I saw darkness. It was late at night. I looked at the clock, it was eight o'clock. I mumbled, "Boy, I shouldn't have slept this long."

I washed up, took the dog out for a few minutes, and rushed to the hospital to see my mother. Walking down the corridor to my mother's room, I ran into my Aunt Lilli. She had a peculiar look on her face.

I asked her, "Is my mother out of the anesthesia yet?" Shaking her fist at me she retorted, "Your mother's dead and it's all your fault. You were a lousy son. You made your mother die by herself, like a dog in the street. I put this curse on you, the same thing is going to happen you."

Shocked, I stepped back, "What do you mean, what happened? They told me everything was fine."

She said, "Where were you all day? Why weren't you here with your mother?"

I began to shake, "I was here. I spent all night with her in the recovery room."

She said, "I don't want to hear anything you got to say. You're no good, you're rotten. I never want to hear from you or see you again. You are a lousy son."

Now my Aunt Lilli never had all her marbles. So I tried to rationalize that she really didn't mean what she said and was just upset by my mother's death. Only half comprehending the fact that my mother had died, I left and drove slowly, numbly, home.

A few weeks after that I got a phone call from my aunt. I was glad to hear from her, after all she was my godmother, she was the one who was supposed to take care of me in case anything happened to my parents. I thought she was calling to apologize for her strange behavior at the hospital. She had said a lot of other weird things too, like her childhood was dead now that my mother was dead. I thought she acted disoriented.

She asked, "What are you doing?"

I replied, "Well, I'm trying to put my mother's and father's clothes together and give them away to the Salvation Army."

Then she said, "Are you going to be there?"

I answered, "Yeah, I'm going to be here."

She said, "Good, I'm coming right over."

Aunt Lilli didn't like to ride the train. Nevertheless, this one time she took the train all the way from the Bronx, where she lived. About an hour later, she got to my apartment and asked, "What are you doing?"

I said, "I told you, I'm trying to put all of my mother's and father's clothes together, and give them to charity."

She made her way to my mother and father's bedroom and sat on the bed. Then she said, "Go to the kitchen and get me a glass of water."

I said, "Okay," got her a drink and gave it to her.

She drank about a mouthful of it, put the glass on top of the dresser and asked, "You're putting all your mother's and father's stuff in order?"

I said, "Yeah."

She said, "Good," then she got up and left.

I thought this was peculiar. "She comes to help me, stays in my apartment about five minutes, and goes?"

I continued gathering my mother and father's things. Then I went to the dresser where my mother kept a special jar with my father's and her wedding rings. Surprised, I noticed the top was off of the jar and the wedding rings were missing. The only one who had been in the bedroom near the jar was my Aunt Lilli.

I waited about an hour, then I called Aunt Lilli. As soon as she heard my voice she hung up on me. So I called my Cousin Jill and I said, "I think Aunt Lilli took my mother's and father's wedding rings."

She said, "Why would she do that?"

I said, "I don't know, she was in my apartment five minutes and left."

I told her what happened at the hospital and Jill said, "Look, I'll find out what is going on. Call me back in about five minutes."

A few minutes later I called her back. Jill answered, "Yeah, Aunt Lilli took the wedding rings. She's just holding them for safekeeping."

I said, "Look, I was planning on putting them in the safety deposit box."

Jill said, "Well, I'll tell you right now she's not going to give them back to you."

I said, "Alright, I'll deal with her later." As it turned out, my Aunt Lilli would never give back the wedding rings, regardless of how many times I asked her. Also, after that she managed to tell everyone I might know that I was a lousy son and made my mother die by herself, like a dog in the street.

* * *

Reliving that whole scene, I started to think that it could be the reason Jill wasn't going to help me.

Since I was in Little Italy, and I was an Italian Catholic, I decided to go to one of the local churches and see if I could get some help there— maybe food, a place to stay, or advice. There was a church right near by, I headed for it. A service was going on in Italian. I waited for the service to end, then I approached the priest and said, "Can I talk to you for a bit?"

He spoke with a strong Italian accent, "Follow me to my office."

"Look, I need a place to stay," I said. "Can you let me sleep in the basement of the church or in the rectory somewhere?"

He replied, "No, we have no room for you."

I asked, "Well, can I at least go in the church and pray?" Staring at me, he reluctantly agreed. I went back to the church and I started to pray.

The other people in the church obviously didn't like the fact that I was there. They pointed at me and made me feel uncomfortable; so I went outside. There, waiting for me, was another bunch of people. They told me, "Now look, get out of this neighborhood."

This was the first time I encountered what I call "a block association," for lack of a better name. They are vigilante groups that appoint themselves the law in their neighborhood to remove undesirables (the Homeless). These groups are never smaller than twenty-five people and sometimes are composed of hundreds of people. First, they tell you to move and then they follow you to the border line of their neighborhood. They throw things at you, and hit you with bats, and even kill you if you don't get out. Cops who see them look the other way, and even shut off the police call boxes in the street.

I said, "Wait a second. I'm doing no harm. I'm not bothering anybody. What do you mean get out of this neighborhood? I'm Italian. This is an Italian neighborhood." I argued with them, but it was really pointless. They already had their minds made up.

They chased me out of the neighborhood, shouting threats never to come back to there for any reason or else I would be beaten up or killed. I ran as quickly as possible until I got onto the Bronx River Parkway. Once there, I breathed a sigh of relief, knowing that the people following me on foot would not come on the Parkway after me.

Then I made my way to the Bruckner Boulevard Expressway, where I started to think about another friend, John. He owned a pizza place on 149th Street and St. Ann's Avenue in the Bronx. I figured that with John, I'd be able to get some food for sure, and maybe he'd give me an empty apartment to stay in for a couple of days. As I got off Bruckner Boulevard onto 149th Street, I spotted another block association waiting for me. They started to chase me.

They didn't know where I was going, but I did. It was almost like being in one of the old Cowboy and Indian movies, where you double back on your trail to lose people who are following you. Well, I walked one way and came back another way, and then I went around in a circle until I got to John's pizza place.

Unfortunately, the pizza place was closed. John owned the building, but I knew he didn't live there. I managed to sneak in without anybody from the block association seeing me. I climbed all the way up to the roof. (My dog was pretty tired out and he was panting heavily. I had to carry him up the last few flights of stairs of the fifth-floor walkup.)

Fearful, I kept looking around for any signs of people. I hoped no one had heard my footsteps creaking up the stairs. I shuddered when C.T. barked a few times. At the top, in front of me, were two big steel doors. They were chained shut and nearby was a large piece of foam rubber. It looked like someone had been sleeping there.

I sat down on the foam rubber with my dog next to me. The sounds of people walking in and out of their apartments filtered up and I kept wondering if they heard me or C.T. I tried to relax because I knew that nobody could go out onto the roof. The doors were locked. I figured my best bet would be to wait for John to open up the pizza place the next morning, and then see if he could help.

Making myself as comfortable as possible, I fell asleep. I must have slept several hours, when I heard loud noises in the street. Sleepily, I rubbed my eyes and sat up. There were windows at the landing in front of the roof steps. Getting up, I walked over to peer out. I couldn't see anything, because they were heavily frosted. Finally, I managed to open one up a crack and peeked out the window. There was a lineup of block association members. I looked up. There was just a hint of light in the sky. People were circling around—somehow I knew they were looking for me. It was like a manhunt out to catch a dangerous criminal like Machine Gun Kelly or John Dillinger. Nothing happened, so I waited.

About fifteen minutes later I looked out the window again, and the block association wasn't there. I had temporarily given them the slip. I said to myself, "Good, I fooled them." Lying back down, I went to sleep again. The next thing I knew, I opened my eyes and saw daylight. I didn't know what time it was; so I decided to wait until I saw the other businesses on the block opening. That would be the time to see if John was in the pizza place.

I sat there waiting and waiting. Then I heard footsteps on the stairs. When the person got to the top floor, he continued to walk up the steps towards the roof. I took a deep breath and exhaled. It turned out to be my friend John. Before he recognized me he said, "Hey look, you got to leave, you can't stay here."

I answered, "Hey, it's Joe."

Surprised he replied, "Oh Joe, I didn't recognize you. What are you doing here?"

I said, "I was waiting for you. I wasn't sure if the pizza place was opened yet."

His eyes widened as he scrutinized me, "What are you doing hanging out in the hallway. You know, I got complaints from the people in the building that somebody was up here."

Ashamed, I looked away and said, "I needed a place to stay. I got evicted from my apartment, I don't have any real money to go live anywhere. I know that you own the building and thought you might have a few empty apartments, maybe you could let me stay in one for a few days. And I knew you wouldn't have me locked up for hanging out in the hallway waiting for you."

He said, "Joe, I'd never call the cops and have you locked up, but you can't stay here. You can't make a career of sleeping on a piece of foam rubber near the roof."

I said, "I know I can't."

He said, "Take your time, get yourself together, then come down to the pizza place. You can have some breakfast and we'll talk about it."

I said, "Okay, Joe." Then he went back downstairs. I got my things together and went downstairs to the pizza place. I told John about all the troubles I was having.

He said, "Joe, have some breakfast." He paused; "There are two empty apartments in the building. My son is going to live in one of them, and the other is in really bad shape. It won't be ready for a couple of weeks and you can't go in there now, because it's really a mess and people will be in there working, fixing it up."

He dug in his pocket, gave me ten bucks, and said, "Look, you know a lot of people. See if someone can put you up for a couple of weeks, then come back and talk to me and maybe we can work out some kind of a deal. If you get hungry and want some food, just come by the pizza place, and you got the food and maybe a couple of bucks too. Don't be shy, come back anytime you want. But remember, you can't make a career out of sleeping in hallways."

I said, "Yeah, I know I can't."

So I left the pizza place and thought of another friend who owned a restaurant nearby. His name was Paul. It was the same story when I saw Paul. He gave me some money and food but not a place to stay. I left his restaurant—again I had gotten no help. I started to walk up Willis Avenue. By then it was late afternoon and most of the block association people seemed to have lost interest in me. I kept walking up Willis Avenue and then I passed 141st Street, the place where my mother used to have a beauty parlor. She called it the Shamrock Beauty Parlor. I started to think about my mother and my relationship with her.

3
The Past, The Present

---

*M*y mother half loved me, half hated me. I was what you would call a change-of-life baby, born when my mother was thirty-seven years old and my father was forty-five. Sometimes, my mother resented me because she had worked as a beautician since she was very young, and it had been a long time before she could afford to buy her own business. Finally, she got a beauty parlor on 141st Street and Willis Avenue in the Bronx. She was very proud of it.

However, when I was born, my father told her

she would have to sell the beauty parlor, stay home and take care of me, because I was more important than a beauty parlor. And what drove her even more crazy was that after she sold the beauty parlor to her partner, the City decided to knock down the whole row of buildings on Willis Avenue and put a Project there. They paid her former partner about five times as much money as she had paid my mother for buying my mother's part of the business.

Years later, when I found all this out, it helped explain a lot of things to me. For instance, when I was a child, the way my mother sometimes ignored me.

Now, my mother was a very good beautician. She had quite a large following. After she had sold her share in the beauty parlor, she started to take customers in our house. She was very busy and, as a result, she neglected me. My mother never used to like to get up early in the morning. She would sleep until 11 a.m. Then her customers would begin to come over to the house, and she used to do their hair.

Often, she would not take me to school. I guess she rationalized, well, it was only the first grade, or second grade, whatever I was in, it wasn't that important. When the school balked about my absences, she would go over and sweet talk the teachers give them some b.s. One way or the other, she would manage to quiet things down and I would be passed to the next grade.

I wasn't complaining about it; I thought she

42

was doing me a favor. What child wants to go to school? Certainly *I* didn't. But her excuses only worked for the lower grades. As I started to get up in the fourth and fifth grades, the school really got upset that I was always absent. They would send a truant officer up to my house to find out why I wasn't in school. They even brought my mother to court, and were going to take me away from her.

When my father found out about it, he went crazy. He really laid down the law. And from that point on, he made sure I went to school every day, and used to call up to school to make sure I was there.

Well, that made my mother's and father's relationship worsen. They were arguing a lot anyway. (My mother always blamed me for that also.) Then, all of a sudden, my mother disappeared. She went to Florida because she didn't like the cold weather, and worked as a beautician.

She left me and my father alone all winter long. I would go to school alone (by that time I was old enough), come home, do my homework, cook for my father, and watch a little television. Then I'd go to bed. As a result, I really didn't have too many friends.

Though my mother was very peculiar sometimes, she did love us. I remember at my father's funeral, she couldn't believe that he was gone. My father used to like playing practical jokes, and the last night before the funeral, she kept calling his name and shaking his arm, saying, "Get up, wake up! Wake up! Stop joking around." She couldn't accept the fact that he'd actually died, because my father was so active, so alive.

After I passed the building where her beauty parlor used to be, it was getting late in the afternoon and I was hungry. I got food in one of the grocery stores on Willis Avenue and looked for a place where I could sit down and eat. On Willis Avenue, there are plenty of burned-out buildings. I decided to choose one in which I could at least find some shelter, eat, and maybe spend the night.

There was a three-story brownstone building that looked the least dilapidated. Inside, I found an apartment that was habitable. It had a door I could close and wedge something against, so nobody could break in. I looked around, trying to take in what had happened to me, how I had ended up on the street.

I felt cold, so I managed to find a sunny window, opened it and let the sun in. Drinking some of the milk and eating a few of the cookies I had bought, I patted my dog and gave him some. I was just sitting there, trying to get warm, thinking of what I was going to do next, when C.T. began barking.

He had spotted a pigeon on the ledge. All of a sudden, he jumped up, pounced on the bird, and killed it. Grasping the pigeon in his mouth, he chewed on it a little bit, and then brought it over to me. It was as if he was telling me, "Here is some good food, some protein. Let those cookies go. Eat something healthy."

"C.T.," I scolded the dog, "you know you shouldn't have done that." That was the first time I really saw my dog kill anything.

Near the kitchen window of our old apartment was a roof. Sometimes my dog would run after the pigeons who perched on it. And he loved to chase them, but he never *killed* anything. But then, in all the time he was living with me, he never had been really hungry. Even now, he didn't kill for himself, because after he killed the pigeon, he brought it over to me. So it really was a compassionate move that he made.

I continued to sit there. A few minutes later, the door started to rattle. A guy looking like a drug addict, with steely eyes and a big knife in his hand, burst into the apartment.

I grabbed my dog and put him behind me, "Stay C.T.," I said firmly.

The guy with the knife walked toward me. I looked around for something to defend myself with. Suddenly the guy stopped, looked at me and looked at my dog. Then he walked to the window and crawled through onto the fire escape outside.

I heard loud, metallic noises; I think he was

trying to cut away some pipe or copper he could sell. I sat there thinking outloud, "Is this guy going to come back and decide he wants to kill me?" Then I mumbled, "Let me get out of this place."

I remembered a big church school cafeteria complex on Alexander Avenue in the Bronx. They used to feed the children there at lunchtime. I thought I'd go to the church and see if I could get some help.

4

The Wild Dogs of the Bronx

I left C.T. outside the red brick building and, hurry-ing in, I asked the priest for sanctuary, like Quasimodo in the movie, *The Hunchback of Notre Dame*, when he asked the priest for sanctuary, safety, and protection.

This priest said, "We don't do that anymore," and handed me a package of cookies. Then he showed me to the door and told me how to take a subway to the Men's Shelter on East Third Street. I'd heard a lot of bad stories about that place and decided to pass on his suggestion.

I trudged onward. On Alexandria Avenue (which is only about five blocks long), I found a police precinct. I thought I'd sit on the stone steps in front of the precinct; I figured I'd be safe there. I was wrong again.

As I sat there, a couple of guys from the block association walked up. They must have had some kind of agreement with the cops, because the cops would do nothing to help me. They wouldn't let me get murdered, but nevertheless they let the block association chase me and make me move.

I started walking again about eleven p.m.—the chase was on. I tried to duck into a couple of grocery stores that I knew about from my earlier trips to the Bronx. They were supposed to be open twenty-four hours a day. But as soon as the chase started, they closed; so there was nowhere to hide from the people in the block associations. I kept on the move, telling myself, "Let me get out of the Bronx and try Manhattan."

After I reached Manhattan, I finally found refuge in a building on Lexington Avenue and 109th Street. I started to think that some of the trouble I was having was probably from going into bad neighborhoods. I decided to try to find help in better neighborhoods. I figured that you can't find a better neighborhood than 86th Street near Central Park, so that's where I went.

I decided to go into Central Park, in spite of all the muggers. After all, muggers would not bother me; I had nothing to steal. The people in the neighborhood would be scared of the muggers in the Park after dark. And the rich would stay in their houses counting their money, not bug me.

Now this was really the wrong idea. First of all, the Park is so heavily landscaped, there is actually no place to hide. Also, the rich people around the neighborhood—the lawyers, the Wall Street types—objected to my being in the Park. Two blue-suited guys from the block association walked through the Park and then strode into the boathouse parking lot on 86th Street. They told the cops in a squad car that was parked there, "There's this creepy guy in the park."

The cops responded, "What do you want us to do, arrest him?"

The blue suits said, "No, no, leave it to us."

Once I overheard this remark I knew something was going to happen, and I was right. About two o'clock in the morning, a bunch of men in white uniforms with croquet mallets in their hands, rode English racer bicycles into the park. They started swinging the mallets and chased me out of the park, following me 'til I was out of their neighborhood.

I kept running. Around 42nd Street, near the United Nations Building, I stopped. Breathless and trembling, I slipped into the shadows, figuring there was nobody around at that time of night to bother me but I was wrong, there was a different block association lurking nearby.

This time the people stalked me in cars, circling and throwing rocks and bottles. Looking around for something to defend myself with, I saw some police barricades stored outside the building. I grabbed the barricades, and piled them up like blocks so the cars could not get near me. Now, anyone who really wanted me had to get to me on foot.

It was almost three, and there were only a few people around. I figured they'd think twice before venturing out of their cars. I murmured, "Good, I've got them stumped."

However, I didn't have them stumped for long. Pretty soon a blue sedan pulled up, a tall, muscular guy got out, walked over to me and snarled, "Get out of here".

I replied, "What do you mean, get out of here? Who are you?"

Then he pulled out his wallet and showed me a badge. He was a police detective. He tightened his lips and repeated loudly, "Get out of here. And if you come back—we're not going to arrest you. We're going to beat you up and put you in the hospital or Boot Hill."

Taking him at his word, I left and tried all over the East Side and West Side of Manhattan. No luck. No refuge. Desperate, I whispered, "Where am I going to go now?" I decided that since the Bronx had always been luckier for me, I should try it again.

I continued walking, because no bus would take me with my dog—and the subway was no good for me because I did not know where I was going. I kept searching for a place that had no people around—perhaps a burned-out building I could stay in.

My feet and legs ached. Even the pads on the bottom of my dog's paws were cracking and raw, and he was limping.

We trudged back to the Bronx. Though it was about three a.m., it wasn't that cold out. I sat on the stoop of a burned-out building, trying to catch my breath and get my mind together.

I glanced at the sky. The weather was strange. The clouds were dark and heavy. Fog hung in the air like a shroud. It looked more like London in the old monster movies. I expected werewolves and vampires to come out of the fog, growling and snarling, saliva dripping out of their mouths.

All the lamps around me had burned out, although I could see dim lights about two blocks away. I turned to look at C.T., but I could only see his silhouette as he jumped up and started to sniff the air. Droplets of water were coming out of his glistening-wet black nose.

He put his hackles up (that is where the little fur on his back stood up). He seemed to be staring down the block into the fog. I knew his sense of hearing and smell were far more acute than mine and he must have perceived some kind of danger for me or him. In another minute he stood and pointed like a hunting dog. Then I heard a loud rattling noise.

Looking around, I saw a gigantic shadow looming up out of the fog. It didn't look human; it was

51

standing up on its hind legs. I whispered to myself,
"Maybe there are really werewolves or vampires,
and I have found one in the Bronx." Slowly, the
thing came toward me. I began to shake. Then I
murmured, "What a way to die. To be eaten by a
werewolf or have all my blood sucked out by a vam-
pire."

Finally, as the shape edged closer, I saw it was
just another guy living in the street. He really looked
a mess. On his back he carried black plastic bags.
Because of them, he was all hunched over, walking
in a crazy way because his toes were coming out of
his shoes. For a moment he stood still and stared at
me curiously, and I stared back at him. Then he
turned away and kept going. My dog barely glanced
at him. His senses were trained on something else.

I looked off in the distance. Something else
must be coming. Suddenly, out of the fog, they appeared, the wild dogs of the Bronx. There must have
been fifteen or twenty. The leader of the pack, his
tail sticking up high in the air and curled around,
came over and scrutinized us.

Now, my dog never knew fear, because the only
thing I ever did to punish him was put peanut butter
on his paw. C.T. was spoiled and fearless.

Unfortunately, this dog was huge. The mongrel
started to growl and bare his fangs. Then, my dog
started to attack. C.T. was over ten-years old, attacking a dog four times his size. I had my hands full
trying to stop my dog from fighting with all the dogs

in the pack. Finally, I calmed him down and we got away.

The next night we got into a building and managed to get some sleep. But those wild dogs of the Bronx kept on being a problem. Many nights I had to protect myself, and C.T. too.

After about a month, I said to myself, "There has got to be a way out of this mess. I'm going nowhere, and I'm going nowhere in a hurry. The few bucks I have will be running out real soon. Then how will I eat?"

I remembered something from driver's education in high school. On the highway, truck drivers will stop and help, if they think you need it. So I went to a place on 138th Street where you can get onto the Major Deegan Highway. In the middle of the road where there is a divider rail, land and grass, I sat down on the grass with my dog in my arms. I waved at the trucks as they went by. I must have stayed there four or five hours. No trucks stopped. As a matter of fact, a few cars tried to jump the divider to hit me and my dog. The idea was a wasted effort. I got up and started to get off the highway.

At this point, my dog could hardly walk. Possibly it was old age; or the lack of food and the fact he was not sleeping most nights, because C.T. would guard me as I slept. Finally, I half pulled, half carried him off the highway and was sitting on this little mountain off to the side. I began to stroke C.T., trying to get him to go to sleep so he could get his strength back. Then I was going to bring him to the Animal Medical Center in Manhattan for treatment. I still had an open charge account with them, so there wouldn't be any financial problem for me.

Suddenly, some people from another block association started to chase us. I tried to get C.T. to move, but he couldn't. I knew I couldn't carry him for any distance, since he weighed about fifty pounds. I decided the only way to get him medical treatment or keep him with me would be to find a milk box, tie him in it, then drag the box with a rope I carried in my pocket.

Trying to formulate a plan quickly, I said, "They're after me, not my dog. I'll try to tie him up as best I can. See if I can lead the block association in a different direction, find a milk box, circle around, and get my dog back." That's just what I did. I came back with a milk box just after daybreak, but my dog was gone.

I walked the whole neighborhood asking about my dog. Nobody had seen him. Maybe he bit through the rope and came looking for me. Maybe he joined a dog pack. I looked everywhere for him. I hope God forgives me and I hope my dog forgives me; if there is a place he can hear me. Many times I think about my dog and chills run up my spine. As always in life, anytime I show bad judgment or make a mistake, I've had to pay for it. This time I lost my best friend and a piece of my manhood.

I kept looking for my dog through three days of driving rain. During this time, I was chased by numerous block associations and was constantly on my feet, with no food and very little to drink. Every time I went into a grocery store, some block association members would follow me and tell the owner to refuse to sell me food. They always threatened that if he did, the block association would tell people in the neighborhood to boycott his store.

By then I was soaked through and through. My ripped clothes felt heavy as I walked because they were soaked. Rain water beat down on my head, and dripped into my eyes, making them red and raw.

At the end of the third day I kept falling and couldn't focus my eyes anymore. I could hardly keep going. But I had to find shelter and find my dog. Every time I found refuge in an apartment building with people living in it, the block association would contact the super and he would kick me out. Or if I darted into a burned-out building, the block association would follow me up and chase me out with baseball bats, jack handles, etc. I knew my body couldn't take much more punishment. I had to do something quickly.

I tried to assess my options: If I tried violence, there were hundreds of people against me and I'd lose. If I tried passive resistance, they would push me out bodily. I was in a no-win situation. The only thing I had remaining was my brain—what was left of it.

Now, at rush hour, I found myself in the Bronx near 174th Street on Boyton Avenue, close to the

Cross-Bronx Expressway. I knew that place—one drop of rain, and there would be traffic backed up for miles. So I got on the Cross-Bronx Expressway and the block association, in cars, followed. Bingo; I had led them into a traffic jam and they were stuck!

I darted across traffic and got off the Cross-Bronx Expressway somewhere near Webster Avenue. I trudged down Webster towards 149th Street. Looking around I saw no one and gave a heavy sigh, I thought I had shaken the block association. They must have called ahead by telephone or used their C.B.'s (Citizens Band Radios), because within minutes, cars began chasing me. The rain kept coming down. If I wanted to survive, I had to keep going.

Finally, I got to 149th and Brook Avenue. There was a big field covering one square block, where buildings had been knocked down. Huge weeds about six to eight feet high covered the field like a jungle. A steel fence surrounded it, but there were holes in it. I murmured, "Let me get in there and hide in the brush like an animal. The foliage was so heavy that in some spots no rain could penetrate. I found a dry piece of ground within the foliage where nobody from the street could see me and lay down. It was the first time I'd been off my feet for three days. Slowly, I began to relax.

God must have been with me, because as I looked up at the dark, clouded sky, it started to clear. The rain stopped and the sun came out. I moved to the middle of the lot where the sun shone the strongest, took off some of my wet clothes and shoes, then hung them on the branches of the weeds to dry. I cleaned my feet as best as I could. Water blisters clustered upon the soles of my feet; they really hurt, but I knew you were not supposed to break them. I left them alone. Stretching out, I half fell asleep, but I knew I couldn't sleep soundly, I had to keep alert.

A little later, I peered through the weeds and saw people in their cars, circling the block. After a while they parked. There must have been twenty-five cars. Some of the men from the block association got out of their cars and began talking. I could hear loud voices, but I couldn't make out what they were saying. They kept shaking their heads like they didn't know what to do.

I knew they wouldn't come in after me. In a situation like that I could very easily ambush them and get the drop on them. These guys are only brave when the odds are one hundred to one. Face to face they won't do anything.

I sat up trying to anticipate what their next moves were going to be. It wasn't long before I knew. They had gathered some newspapers and were trying to light a fire. They were going to try to burn me up or out. The foliage was too wet and they struck out, then got disgusted, but they kept talking. I thought that was fine—let them talk because I knew they weren't going to be able to get me out as long as the foliage was wet.

About half an hour later I saw some men coming down the block with big mongrel dogs on leashes. They unfastened them and sent the dogs in after me, trying to flush me out, just like hunters flush out birds, rabbits, or some other prey. But one thing they didn't know was that I have a special relationship with dogs. We get along. (Now, these were not professionally-trained, kill-on-command watchdogs. They were just regular dogs, pets that people had.)

First one, then more dogs came. They bared their teeth and growled at me. I started softly talking to them.

Dogs seldom attack without reason. These same dogs, if I walked into the place where they were living, would probably attack me to protect their home, but in the street it's all different. They were there just to play, and enjoy themselves. Now if I had run, they would have followed me and chewed me up, 'cause dogs love to chase. So I just kept talking during the next hour or so. But then about ten or fifteen big dogs joined the pack encircling me.

They cocked their heads back and forth as I continued talking to them. Then I got a couple of dogs to come near me and I started to pet them. I got them to lie down and roll over on their backs, and I started rubbing their chests, scratching them on the bottom of their jaws. They were wagging their tails and having a good time. They couldn't have been happier.

By then their masters were really going crazy because they didn't know what had happened to the dogs. They must have thought I had killed them, because they could not hear or see them. And when they called, the dogs wouldn't go back. I put my clothes back on, enjoying the sun beating down on me. When a couple of dogs lay down beside me, I could feel the warmth from their bodies where they touched me, and hoped they did not have fleas. I was just relaxing, taking it easy, drying out and getting my thoughts together; getting some enjoyment out of watching their masters going crazy. I knew it could not last indefinitely, but I wanted to enjoy it as long as I could.

Half asleep, I heard a noise, opened my eyes, and saw a sign hanger. (If you've ever seen a cherry-picker with the fire department, it has a hook and ladder with a bucket at the end of the ladder. A man can get in the bucket. Sign hangers use a similar set-up to hang signs).

The man in the bucket had been sent to spot me because the buildings around there were burnt up too badly for any of the block association's members to get on the roofs. Seeing me, he directed the block association in. About fifty of them ran into the field with baseball bats, tire irons, and pipes in their hands.

One had a Bible in one hand and a stick in the other. He must have been some kind of minister or deacon. He looked straight at me and the expression on his face was one of pure hatred. Strangely, the hatred wasn't for me. It was for his dog, and he started to beat the poor animal mercilessly.

A group of men stood over me, threatening that if they found me again in the neighborhood, I would get my head bashed in, or be killed. I left. I had had six or seven hours of rest and felt better. My clothes had dried out somewhat, but my shoes were still wet and soggy.

Then I thought, "There's a whole row of burned-out buildings close by, between Willis and Brook Avenues. If I can get into one of these buildings, maybe no one will be able to find me. I can finish drying out and rest some more."

The first buildings I found were in really bad shape. The staircases and floors were all rotten, and several times I almost fell through them. I kept searching for a building that wasn't too bad to stay in. When I saw a grocery store, I decided to snatch the opportunity to get some food before some block association spotted me again.

I got the food just in the nick of time! As I was coming out of the store, one of the block association members drove his car around the corner, spotted me, and started to follow me. I knew that it wouldn't be long before he called some of his friends on his C.B.; so I went into a different row of burned-out buildings.

One looked better than the rest and slowly I walked up the steps, searching for an apartment where I could eat my food in peace and quiet. Suddenly, halfway up, chills ran up and down my spine. My head snapped back. I could not move. A vision of my dog, C.T., filled my mind. There seemed to be an invisible barrier stopping me from going up the staircase. So I walked down to the landing below and sat on a window sill. I didn't feel like eating anymore and I started down the steps to the street.

Then I looked up at the bottom of the staircase I had been trying to walk up. I could see that all the braces which held the top half of the marble steps were rotted away. The steps could never have held my weight. I would have fallen through to the next floor onto the staircase just below, then rolled down the staircase. I could have been hurt really badly.

As I shuddered, I noticed that if I could walk up the flight of steps on the ledge at the bottom of the banister, I would not fall through and could sleep soundly that night. Not only would I be safe but anybody who tried to walk up these steps to get at me would fall through. If that happened, I would wake up, have plenty of time to get out through the fire escape and get away. So that's what I did. On the third floor I found probably the only habitable apartment in the whole row of buildings. I went in and sat down near the fire escape and tried to relax.

A little while later, I heard the same guys who had been chasing me come up the stairs and talk on their C.B.s. Suddenly, all voices stopped as they fell through to the floor below. Loud moans and groans filtered up. Quickly I made my way out the fire escape down to the back yard, because I knew the block association would be really angry now. If they caught me, I would get beaten up or maybe killed.

I climbed through some more buildings and

this time I came out on Willis Avenue. In front of me was a church with an open, black steel gate. The church was closed, but the door to the basement was open. I knocked at the door and there was no answer. So I walked in saying, "Hello, hello, is anybody here?" I knocked at the closed office doors, but there was no answer. Then I heard somebody rattling around. It was a wrinkled old man, probably some kind of watchman.

I asked, "Is there a minister around?"

He gave me a puzzled look and cupped his hand to his ear. I realized he must have been hard of hearing. I began to yell and use hand signals to explain what I wanted. He answered "You don't have to shout. Nobody's here. What can I do for you?"

I said, "I badly need a place to stay."

He said, "Well, the minister isn't here. If you like, you can hang out in the basement and wait for him. I don't know when he'll be back."

"That'll be good," I tried to smile, "that'll be great."

He directed me to waxed and polished wooden steps which led to the basement. Then, from a switch on the wall near the top of the staircase, he turned on the basement light. I looked around. It was a place with heat, hot and cold running water, and even a clock on the wall. It had been a long time since I had been anywhere near a sink that had hot and cold running water. Sighing, I washed my face and hands. The clean, clear water felt great. Feeling like a human being for the first time in days I sat down on a chair and ate the food I had bought earlier.

After I had eaten, I washed the rest of my body. Then I sat down again and cleaned my bleeding, bruised feet the best I could. Afterward, I hung up some of my clothes to dry out near a heating vent. I was hoping that the preacher or minister would not show up for a while.

Tired beyond all I had ever felt, I fell asleep. I really don't know how long I was there. It might have been a day, it might have been longer, but when I woke my body felt much better. My thoughts were clearer.

It was morning. I heard somebody walking down the steps to the basement and saw someone approaching me. He introduced himself as the minister. Then he asked, "Why are you here?"

I replied, "I need a place to live and some food."

He shook his head, "Well, you can't stay here. Go down to the Men's Shelter on East Third Street."

I said, "I got no way of getting there."

He explained, "You take the train," and then he told me how to get there.

I said, "I got no carfare."

He replied, "Well, this is a very poor parish. We can't give you any money. Nevertheless, you're gonna have to leave."

I said, "How about some food?"

He grimaced, "Look, this isn't a restaurant. Please leave." And I left.

I had been kicked out again. My body had benefited from eating and sleeping, but my long-term problem had not changed. Back on my feet, I resumed my search for shelter.

5

Life in the Shelters

I still had nowhere to go. I headed down to the Bowery. Once there, I decided to try the Men's Shelter on East Third Street in Manhattan. The distance was long and I was tired, but I made my way toward it. When my feet started aching again, I sat down on an old suitcase I found in the street near a bus stop. The bus came, and a few people hopped on.

Slowly, I rose and called to the bus driver, "Does this bus go to the Men's Shelter at East Third Street?"

He answered, "Yes, get on."

I added, "I got no car fare."

The bus driver replied, in a jovial Irish brogue, "Don't worry about it, just get on. I'll tell you when to get off." I got inside the bus and we drove off.

After we reached the right place, the driver shouted to me and I got off the bus and started walking. Bums lined the landscape. I must have seen about three block's of homeless people hanging around between the bus stop and the shelter.

Later, I figured out the reason why so many bums were decorating the landscape: Even if you get shelter for a night, you're put out on the street the next morning between six and seven o'clock. Most bums have no money, no place to go. They hang out in doorways, gutters, etc., to kill time until the soup kitchens open for lunch or dinner.

This is why you hear people say they don't want shelters in their neighborhood. It's not the bums' fault. The bums are doing what they gotta do—keeping out of the sun, keeping out of the rain, trying to keep warm, trying to survive.

But the city, church, or private shelters could supply retraining or resources so the homeless would be able to improve their minds or situation; rather than just lie in the street. If shelters altered their purpose from supplying a place to sleep to educating and retraining those who find themselves on the streets, bums wouldn't cause problems to people in the neighborhood. They would be occupied for the better part of the day in a learning environment.

Well, I finally made it to the front of the City Shelter, and walked through a doorway with a lot of bums on each side. I found myself in a big room that was very clean and neat. In front of me were a bunch of glass partitions with signs over them labeled: Welfare, Clothing, etc. I did not know which window I should go to; so I tried the first one, and asked the middle-aged Hispanic man sitting behind it, "How do I get some food and a place to sleep?"

He asked, "You have any identification?"

I answered, "Yes," and showed it to him.

He scanned it for a minute, and gave me two cards. Then he spoke rapidly, with a strong accent. "One card is a meal ticket. Take it to the cafeteria in the basement and get breakfast, lunch, or dinner. It can be used ten times. We also give out clothes a few times a week. The other card is for shelter. You have to take it down the block to the private hotel that is rented by the City in the evening to get a bed. Make sure you get there early to get a bed, because these cards are given to everybody who gets a meal ticket and they are not dated or numbered. We are never sure of how many men will come for shelter on any one night."

"What kind of room will I get?" I asked hesitantly.

Flashing me an annoyed look he answered, "You do not get a room, you get a bed in a dormitory if you are early. If you are late, you are out of luck." Then he added, "Now go sit outside and wait 'til we open the cafeteria for lunch."

I said, "How will I know when it is time to come inside for lunch? I have no watch."

He gave a slight sigh, "When it's lunch time you'll know it, don't worry."

I nodded slowly, gratefully, "Okay, thank you." Then I went outside and sat down on the sidewalk, just like all the other bums.

As I sat there I started to feel people looking at me. It felt the way a beautiful woman must feel when she wears a mini-skirt and has nice legs, and somebody is looking her up and down, desiring what she has. I felt shocked at being eyed-up. Now I'm not a pretty woman, and I'm not a particularly handsome guy. Finally, I figured out that I was being looked up and down by the other bums because they could tell I was a rookie derelict. This meant that I probably had luxury items on me, like cigarettes, matches, possibly some money.

I couldn't read their minds; but I could read their eyes, which were saying, "Well, let's see how we can get something off this guy." I was getting more nervous by the minute; so I lit up a cigarette. As soon as I did, the other bums moved closer to me so they could smell the smoke. Their noses twitched as they inhaled. They looked like they were helping me smoke the cigarette. More agitated, I took a deep breath then ground the cigarette out.

They didn't move. My hands were shaking; so I took out another cigarette and lit it up. A stringy-haired, toothless bum came over to me and said, "You ain't got no respect. You ain't got no smarts."

I asked, "What do you mean?"

He said, "You're wasting matches."

I said, "What do you mean I'm wasting matches?"

He said, "When you light up a cigarette, you don't have to use a whole match. What you do is rip the match down lengthwise. Then you put your finger over it as you're striking it on the book of matches. You can use that same match twice, and you don't run out of matches so fast." He leaned his face toward me.

I noticed the big blisters on his lips and wondered how he'd gotten them. I didn't ask. I just nodded and said, "Okay, thank you." Finishing the cigarette, I threw it away but I didn't duck it out.

This guy had an old election medal pinned on his shirt. He took it off and stuck the pin part of the medal into the cigarette on the floor, picked it up, and started to puff. There wasn't much left. I smoke a non-filter brand but he smoked it until it burned his lips. I grimaced, and realized that he had gotten the blisters on his lips from smoking other people's butts.

I turned away and started talking to the man I

was sitting next to. He had a patch covering one of his eyes. I asked him, "What's the hotel like?"

"Well," he told me, "the bums call the guard who works there 'Stromboli.'" (That was the evil puppeteer who kidnapped Pinnochio in the fairy tale.) "He continually curses them out. On cold days he likes to throw bums into the shower with all their clothes on, then push them into the street." He pointed to a man with one arm sitting on a car and said, "His name is Marty. Stromboli did that."

I said "Did what?"

He said, "He made that guy lose his arm."

I asked, "How?"

He answered, "I just told you what Stromboli likes to do. One day he put Marty in the shower with all his clothes on, then threw him in the street, soaking wet. That day it was close to zero. At night, Marty tried to sleep in a doorway and the next thing he knew, a doctor was telling him he had to cut off his arm. I even heard Stromboli joke to one of his friends that he did Marty a favor because afterwards Marty got cleaned up and lived in a hotel for about a year, until Welfare closed his case and Marty had to come back down here."

I shook my head, "How come Stromboli did not get fired?"

The bum flashed me a crooked smile. "You've got a lot to learn," he said, got up, and walked away toward another group of bums who were sitting on a car away from everybody else.

I didn't move, just sat there. Looking around, I

saw other bums, derelicts with all kinds of deformities. Compared to them, my appearance was really not that bad even though my clothing was dirty and messed up; I had all my body parts and was not disfigured. There were guys in rags; moreover, some were all twisted up, hunched over, and had dirt all over them that looked like it was part of their skin.

I looked down at my own clothing and realized most of my clothes was in fairly good shape. At least they didn't have big holes. But one part of my clothes, the most important part—my shoes—were really in bad shape. They had holes in the sides. Through the holes, I could see my socks—dried blood was crusted on them oozing from my bleeding feet.

I remembered the man who gave me the meal ticket saying they gave out used clothing a few times a week. I thought, "I need to get some shoes." I started wondering, "But where do these people get used shoes?" Then I remembered that when my parents died, I had given away all their clothing to charitable organizations. I assumed that's where these people got most of their clothing.

Despair filled me. Not long ago I had been a person who had been able to give to others. Now I was one of those others. I shook off my dark thoughts. If I were to survive I had to move forward, forget about the past.

At least I had the other ticket, good for a hotel at which to sleep. I went down the block to look at it. It was a small gray building covered with graffiti,

right near a gas station. The smell of gas fumes per-
meated the air. I shuddered. Some of the burned-
out buildings at which I had stayed in the Bronx
looked better.

Then I walked back to the shelter and looked
again at the group of men waiting with me. The guy
with the patch over his eye stood with some others,
talking and staring at me hard. The men, who were
bunched in a group, seemed to be part of a clique.
Their heads were bent together as if they were con-
spirators planning something.

As they were talking, a bum with black, caked-
together hair passed them carrying a full box of
donuts he was just opening up. A muscular bum in
the group strode over to him and demanded, "Give
me a donut."

The man with the donuts said, "No."

The muscular guy grabbed the other bum's
hand, bent it back, and pushed him to the ground. A
guard stood outside the doorway of the shelter
watching, but did nothing to stop the intimidation.

After observing that, I started to fear for my life,
sleeping in a large dormitory with all these guys.
They were hungry, broke, and desperate. If I slept
soundly, anything could happen.

I decided to try a private shelter that some of
the churches I'd been to had recommended. It
wasn't that far away, so I walked there. The shelter
was housed in a huge, red brick building that looked
neat and had no graffiti.

Unfortunately, the homeless clustered about its

entrance. One of them, a slight blond man, was sitting down on the sidewalk with his back resting on the building. I asked him, "Is this the way to the shelter?

He answered, "Yes, if you want any more information, go inside and ask."

A paunchy, balding man was sitting at a table blocking the entrance to the shelter. "How do I get food and a place to sleep?" I asked.

"We're going to open the doors in a little while. Come in then and you can have food and possibly get a bed for the night."

I nodded, "All right."

The frustration of it all was beginning to get to me. Sighing, I went outside, got on line with the rest of the bums, and sat down. The guy next to me was a grungy, dark-haired bum with green snake-skin boots. I asked, "Did they give you those boots here? They cost big bucks."

He smiled a bitter smile. "No, I was a rock star and had lots of money." Then he told me his name and mentioned a few of the songs he had done.

I recognized them. Looking at him more intently I said, "I think I've seen you on T.V. How'd you wind up down here?"

He looked off into the distance, "Oh, I've had several problems. One was my vocal cords. And the others were coke and alcohol."

I had to laugh at the ho-hum way he said it. He seemed like a nice guy and we immediately took to each other. As we were talking, they opened the

73

doors of the shelter. All the men got up and strag-
gled inside. I followed them to a big room, the size
of a high school auditorium. I looked around. It was
a strange setting for a church: a bland room, with
no altar (although there were crosses on the wall)—
just bench seats, a stage, and a podium.

A sermon was just beginning. A gray-haired
man without a clerical collar stood behind a podium on the stage, talking into a microphone. His
voice boomed out from speakers on the four walls of
the room. As soon as he finished, another man took
his place and read from the Bible through the same
microphone set-up. He spoke about Jesus and how
Jesus loves you.

Then they introduced their special entertainment for the evening, a bunch of guys with all kinds
of musical instruments. They played rather badly
for about a half an hour. I thought, "These people
can't be musicians." And I was right.

Very soon I learned they were there to confess
to their sins. They had been caught producing and
peddling pornographic movies featuring children,
animals, etc. They freely admitted their sins and
told how after they had been shown the error of
their ways, they'd found salvation.

After the pornography producers spoke, some
of the directors of the shelter played a biblical version of twenty questions with all the bums. "Do you
know who did what?" Like in school, if you knew
the answer, you would raise your hand. This went
on for about an hour.

After that it was time to see who got a bed for that night. All the bums had to stand in a long line against a wall. One at a time, they ushered you into a little cubicle. You were interviewed and asked to show identification. Then you were told to go outside and sit down in the church. Afterward, a few men who worked for the shelter arbitrarily picked men and gave them a little card. (Only about twenty-five percent of the men got a card that entitled them to a bed.)

When they finished giving out the cards, we were told it was time for dinner and to go to the cafeteria in the basement. I walked along with the rock star, we sat down at the same table. Just then, one of the directors of the shelter came over and invited the rock star to their table, where the guests of the night—the musicians, (a/k/a pornography producers)—had already been given seats. At this table, roast beef, fresh vegetables, and fresh-baked bread were served. But the homeless, who crowded the tables in the rest of the room, were given canned clam chowder, which is one of the private shelter's standbys. Now beggars can't be choosers, but I'm allergic to fish. So I had to forget the soup. I was able to get a buttered roll and drank a container of milk, which was certainly better than nothing.

I glanced over to see the directors of the shelter, pornography producers, and rock star enjoying their "lavish" meal. They were all talking and joking around. I didn't speak. I knew I was headed out into the street again, because I did not get a card that

would entitle me to a bed. I drank as much water as
I could, because water in the street is hard to come
by, then put on my coat. The rock star saw me and
he came over, "Aren't you gonna stay here to
night?"

I said, "No, I wasn't one of the chosen few. I
didn't get a card."

He said, "Well, they gave me a card."

I said, "I know, I saw them giving it to you."

Then he said, "You know, this place, I really
don't trust it."

I asked, "Why?"

He answered, "First of all, one of the directors
offered me a deal. He wanted me to lipsync some
records for some kinda concert they might have,
and he offered to pay me five dollars a day. Also, he
said if I followed his directions, I wouldn't have to
shape up to get a bed. I'd get a bed every night."

I said, "You ought to do it; if you ain't got no
money, five dollars a day is a lot."

He said, "Yeah, and I ain't got no money. But
that ain't the weirdest part of it. Remember, the
guys who were talking about being pornography
producers, the ones who said they were reformed?"

I nodded, "Yeah."

He said, "Well, one of them is gay. He wanted
to take me to a hotel tonight." As we were talking,
one of the directors of the shelter passed by. The
rock star went over to him and gave him a hard
time. He said, "Hey, if my friend doesn't stay, I'm
not gonna stay."

He pointed to me. The directors didn't want to lose the rock star, because they were planning all those concerts with him, hoping to make some big bucks. They nonchalantly walked over to one of the other bums to whom they had just given a card, grabbed it out of his hand, then gave it to me. It was a really cruel and rotten thing to do. But I was too tired to object.

Then all the men who had no cards were asked to leave. Afterwards, two brawny men with night-sticks, who worked for the shelter as bouncers, came over to those who stayed and asked to see their cards. A few men said they lost them. The bouncers grabbed them and threw them out. The elect were told to go to the fifth floor to sleep. My feet and legs were in bad shape—it was really an effort to climb steps. I crept up awkwardly. Some of the others hobbled also.

The directors used an elevator. But the home-less, no matter how disabled, were not permitted to use it—even a man with no legs, who looked like his body was cut in half. He got around on something that looked like a skate board. To walk up the steps, he used his arms and hands like legs. When we reached the floor, two of the directors pointed to a large room filled with bunk beds, where we were supposed to sleep. The rock star shook his head, "I've seen enough, I'm heading for the street."

I was too exhausted to be particular, "Alright, look, I'll see you around," I said. He waved and took off.

I looked at the beds and thought, at least I'll get off my feet for a little while. Then they informed us, we were all going to have to take a shower. I sighed and murmured, "Good, I could use one." Then I looked at the shower. It looked like the same kind of set-up they use at the zoo to bathe animals. There were brown colored tile stalls, just like the zoo has, and you were bathed in a group just like animals. "If I had any pride left," I thought, "this would really take it away."

The person doing the bathing was a tiny guy with a hump on his back. He reminded me of the little hunchback man, Fritz, who used to go running around pulling all the electrical switches in the old Frankenstein movies. It was his job to bring the Frankenstein monster to life. This shriveled guy looked just like him. And he had the same kind of mentality.

Sitting around waiting to go in the shower, I looked at some of the men strip down before they went into the shower. The ones with artificial limbs took them off and put them on a bench close to the shower stall entrance where they could watch them. Even artificial limbs can be hocked. I could see a large assortment of bugs coming out of some of the limbs. The bouncers saw them also. They began to search the limbs, plus everybody's clothes and possessions, for drugs and weapons.

Turning away, I watched another guy, who had all his limbs, strip down; he accidentally dropped a book of matches and walked away without seeing them. As soon as he was safely in the shower, another man pounced on the matches. With a big smile on his face he held them up and said "Oh man! A book of matches."

I frowned, "What's the big deal about a book of matches?"

He looked incredulous, "It means I can pick up cigarette butts in the street and I can smoke almost indefinitely. You don't know much yet, do you?"

I shook my head, "Guess not."

That made me realize that when you're a bum, a book of matches can make you feel independently wealthy.

Next, I started talking to a short, stocky man next to me. "I'm here all the time," he observed, running his hand over his balding head.

"How safe is this place?" I asked.

He answered with another question, "Well, how sound do you sleep?"

I said, "I don't know."

He replied, "Well, if you sleep sound, it ain't that safe."

I said, "Well, don't they have guards at night?"

He said, "One guy sits in a chair, then he falls asleep. You got to protect yourself."

As we were talking, a fight broke out between two bums who had just come out of the shower. There were standing in line to get paper night gowns. As we watched, one of the guys brandished a single-edge razor blade which he had hidden in the bottom of a crush-proof box of cigarettes. I gasped as he cut off the ear of the man he was fighting with. The guy who got cut shook his head like a wet dog, trying to get the blood out of the ear he no longer had.

As he shook, his blood splattered all over the place. Reaching his left hand up, he realized he no longer had his ear attached to his head. "Fuck you," he yelled and knelt down frantically searching for it on the floor. Grasping the ear, he tried to put it back on his head.

The man who did the cutting began to run away. He was caught by the bouncers and began to fight them. They hit him over and over in the head with their night sticks. Finally, he fell to the floor unconscious.

The bouncers went over to the man who was cut. One handed him a towel to stop the blood. Then they helped him over to a bench. I heard them ask him for his ear, so they could put it on ice and give it to the doctor in the ambulance when it came. The bum slowly handed it to them. Then he pressed the towel to the side of his head. I continued looking at him as his face turned white and he passed out. A few minutes later, an ambulance and the cops came. Both men were taken away.

After they left, I decided to take a closer look at the beds. The sheets were dirty and had lice on them. Depressed I looked at some of the other bums. I could see myself mirrored in them. That's when the realization of where I was really sank in. I wanted to run away, to leave, because I did not want to be like the bums I saw there. I did not want to give up my membership in the human race, which is what you do if you sleep in one of these places. You become little more than an animal.

I could say it was for my safety's sake that I decided to go back on the street, but it was really more my ego and my self-respect. Until I could get my life back together, it would be the street and brutal, brutal cold weather. Would I be able to survive? I didn't know.

I would have to call on all the strength I had left to get through this winter without staying in a shelter. I felt that if I succeeded, I wouldn't be a bum or a derelict.

We'd already had a few light snow flurries. I knew what the snow felt like on my bruised feet. Worse was the salt they put on the snow to keep people from falling got into the open wounds. Every time I'd step into slush, my feet burned and froze at the same time.

Nevertheless, I had to leave. Walking out of the shelter, I started to go uptown. Passing by newsstands, I could see pictures of thermometers on the front page of the newspapers, along with headlines such as, "Baby, it's cold outside." The mercury read near zero.

Hours later, I found myself on Fourteenth Street. I passed by an appliance store, looked at a clock in the window—it was 11 a.m. As I turned to walk away, I found a big empty cardboard-and-wood carton, the type of box that is used to ship refrigerators. I took the cardboard box and moved it across the street into a nearby park, where all the drug pushers hung out.

The sun came out as I positioned the box in the sun and lay down inside. As the sun shone on me, I stopped shivering and closed my eyes. Half asleep, I could see C.T.'s eyes and nose. His mouth was open, his tongue hung out. The look he was giving me meant danger. I bolted up and started to think about how meat looked when I took it out of my freezer. I would look like that if I fell asleep now. The heat of the sun could go away at anytime—and once asleep, I would never know. There was a good possibility that I wouldn't wake up at all and would freeze to death. If that didn't happen I could wake up in an operating room somewhere, with a doctor saying, "I'm gonna have to cut off your arm or your leg because it's frozen and all the blood vessels have ruptured and turned black." Maybe my dog had given me these ideas. Maybe we did have a mind link, as I once thought.

The sun was seeping into the cardboard box. It felt good, but I knew I couldn't allow myself to fall asleep. I crawled out. I had to keep on the move. I got up and began walking, searching for a place to stay out of the cold—but not a shelter. Somewhere along the line I managed to find a few office buildings in which to keep warm. I still had a little change for a container of milk.

Days later, I wound up around 125th Street and Second Avenue in Manhattan. It was late in the afternoon, I was very tired and it was freezing. I had reached bottom and did not know what to do. The cold weather was really getting to me. I had to make a move. But what? I couldn't figure anything out and looked up to the sky for help. Then, looking down again, I saw a big white cross hanging from an old tenement building and a sign in the window next to it that said "Church."

I made my way to the building where the church was. The church was really a loft. Inside the hall, it was warm and I sat down near a radiator, which was next to a flight of wooden steps that led into the church. Steam hissed from a little silver valve at the side of the radiator. I took off my coat and put it on the radiator for a few minutes. Once my coat got hot I put it on. Never had anything felt so good.

Down the hall, I heard some kind of service going on inside the church. It was being conducted in Spanish, and I didn't know what they were talking about. I decided to relax, get warm, and try to get my thoughts together. I was hoping someone there spoke English. I wondered what I should say when I got to talk to the preacher or minister. Should I ask him for money, food, a place to stay or what? I had been refused so many times.

Suddenly a freezing, wet, burning sensation spread all over my body. Startled, I jumped up. Someone had thrown a huge amount of water with bleach onto me. I was drenched from the top of my head to the bottom of my feet. I looked up the stairs and saw several men standing on the landing. A tall guy, well padded and dressed, had a big steel gray pail in his hand. It was the kind you use to soak and wring out mops. Rollers were attached to the top.

He yelled, "Get out of here. Get out of here!" So I had to leave once again. Within minutes I was back out on the street. Not only was the brutal cold weather near zero, but I was soaked through and through. It was a desperate situation. My eyes couldn't focus. I was seeing double and triple. Moreover, I could hardly stand on my pain-filled feet. I was trembling from weakness, having neither eaten nor slept for a long time. I didn't know how long it had been. I was ready to fall down and give up. Then, magically, I saw my dog, C.T., again.

I could see him, but I could also see through him and he was circling me, trying to get me to follow him. I had no other answers, so even if my mind was playing tricks on me, I decided to obey. I guess I imagined my dog was transferring his animal instincts to me on how to survive the cold.

Like him, all I was at this time was an animal trying to survive. As soon as I began following him, my feet stopped hurting. My clothes were still wet, but I didn't feel the biting cold. I kept walking. He led me into a five-story walk-up that had two private doors. Locks were on them, but they were not fastened. I continued following him up the steps to the fifth floor, then toward an apartment with a steel door. It had no lock and was open.

I looked around. I was inside an apartment

building that had partially burnt down. Some apartments had escaped the fire and still had people living in them. A few apartments were unoccupied, as they had been burnt badly. The apartment into which I wandered had four rooms, but only the two front bedrooms were badly burnt. The kitchen and living room were untouched. Magically, there was steam heat and shelter from the cold. I closed the steel door behind me and wedged a metal rod I found on the floor through the hole. Nobody could get in. I was safe for the first time in weeks.

6

Visions of C.T.

I slept and slept. My state of unconsciousness may
have lasted two or three days or longer. Several
times, I half awakened. One time it was daylight and
the next time it was night. But each time, exhausted,
I fell back into a deep, dreamless sleep. When I finally woke up completely, light streamed through
the windows.

Sitting up, I started to think about seeing my
dog. Had I finally gone crazy or were these visions
something supernatural? Is it true, as some philoso-
phers say—that no brain energy ever dies, it just

goes into the universe, and at times of need it will come to you? Had my dog's energy helped save my life? Was he or his energy guarding me?

Well I don't know too much about those kinds of things; all I know is this—in that room, I could feel my dog by my feet. Even today, though he is dead many years, I still feel his warmth next to me when I sleep.

The old tenement building I found myself in was owned by the New York City Housing Authority. It was patrolled by the Housing police. There were signs all over the hallway leading up the stairs, saying "No trespassing. Trespassers will be prosecuted to the fullest extent of the law." I would have to be careful going out of this apartment and the building to make sure nobody saw me.

I didn't want to get kicked out into the brutal cold or get locked up for trespassing. But I was hungry and thirsty. Somehow I had to get some food and drink. The question was how? The apartment was on the top floor; I would have to walk down five flights of steps to the street. There was a good chance somebody living in this building would hear or see me. Then they would kick me out or call the cops.

Suddenly, I remembered an old tenement building I used to live in. It was connected to most of the other buildings on the block by a common roof. As a child, my friends and I used to play on the roof. We would walk onto one building, then come out any one of five or six other buildings. I crossed my fingers; maybe it was the same in this tenement building. Walking to the door, I pressed my ear against it, heard nobody; so I very carefully tiptoed out of the apartment and climbed up one flight of steps to the roof. Opening the steel door, I peered out.

There were three other roof doors that were open. I was in luck. This building was constructed the same way as the one I remembered. I could come out any one of four buildings that were connected by the same roof. If somebody saw me walking down to the street and told me to get out, I'd go. I could get back through one of the others or if they called the cops, the cops would be looking in the wrong building for me.

Trudging over the roof to one of the other buildings I opened the thick steel door. As I walked in I saw a dark curly-haired young guy getting ready to shoot up some heroin. At the side of the staircase he had a candle burning and he was cooking his dope in a cap from a soda bottle. Something was tied around his arm and his "works" (hypodermic needle) lay by his side.

In a voice which grew louder and louder, he cursed, half in Spanish, half in English. He was really angry—not that I had discovered him, but because he was losing some of his dope through perforations around the side of the bottle cap he was cooking his dope in. And what got him even madder was that he wasn't going to get his full shot of dope anyway, because he did not have enough money to get a full bag. So, he had to get a short bag of dope.

I said, "Yeah, yeah" and kept on walking until I was out of the building. Then I began searching for a grocery store.

Walking along, I passed a station wagon with the tailgate down. In the back was an oven. Inside it, I saw big trays like you bake or cook things in. One of the trays, covered with silver foil, had an outline of a turkey in it. I looked to the left and saw a dish heaped high with chocolate chip cookies covered by plastic wrap. Smacking my lips I murmured, "Wow, somebody's going to have a party." I waited close to the station wagon. A young guy with crewcut hair walked up and reached inside the station wagon. He picked up a tray and started to walk through an open black steel gate that led to the church's basement. I ran after him and asked, "Is there any chance of getting some food?"

He said, "You have to talk to the priest."

I said, "Where's the priest?"

He answered, "He's in the church next door right now, giving a sermon."

I went in. The middle-aged, gray-haired priest was standing at the altar talking to his congregation. He had a warm manner. And he was telling the story in the Bible about the little fishes. "If you cast your bread upon the water to feed the fish," he said, his deep voice resonating through the room, "the fish are going to appreciate this. And if the time of the flood ever comes, the fish will build a mountain for you on the bottom of the ocean that you can stand on. So you won't drown and die. Remember it's better to give than receive."

I mumbled to myself, "This priest, man, he's telling the right story. He's got a kind face and I'm hungry. If I wait until the end of the sermon maybe I can talk to him."

At the end of the sermon, people began leaving the church, I went through the door near the rail, where people kneel to receive holy communion, and started talking to the priest. He motioned to me to follow him into a little room called the Inner Sanctum that was behind the altar. That's where priests have their prayer books and store their robes, then do their serious praying.

I said, "Look I need some food and water and a place to live." He kept staring at me and nodding his head yes, as he took off the white and green silk robe he had worn during the service. I kept talking and talking. Then he motioned, come with me. We left the Inner Sanctum, walked to the back of the church and outside, through the big black steel gate. We passed right by the basement. So I asked the priest, "The food down here?"

He said, "No, no, no. Come with me."

I followed him to a building, next to the basement that is called the rectory (that's where the Catholic priests live).

He said, "Wait outside the rectory door for a few minutes and I'll be right back." He pushed the door open and went in. As I stood there shivering, I

91

could hear him locking it behind him so I couldn't get in. I thought, maybe he's a little scared because of the way I look. I waited and I waited.

"Funny," I murmured, "he said it would only be a couple of minutes." But it was more than a couple of minutes and I mumbled, "Maybe he's trying to find some food and clothes for me."

I blew on my hands which were turning red from the cold, and started to shake. I could see my smoky breath, and my nose began running. I was getting hungrier every minute. I tried to imagine what kind of food he might give me. Perhaps it would be ham, turkey, home-baked cookies, or maybe lasagna, which is one of my favorites. I had all kinds of positive thoughts. Fifteen or twenty minutes passed, maybe a half hour. All was silent.

Then I heard a loud noise. It came from above my head—I looked up. Billows of smoke and water streamed down. I ducked out of the way trying to protect my face with my hands so I wouldn't get hit directly. Despite this, boiling hot water hit my hands. Immediately blisters rose up. Luckily, no water had hit my face, or I would have been burned badly. I stretched my neck to see exactly where the water came from.

It was the very same priest, now holding a big cauldron in his hand, yelling at me, "Get out of here. Get out of here. Don't come back."

Discouraged, I decided to find a store and get some food with the couple of bucks I had left. At the grocery, I got a bottle of water, loaf of bread, milk, and cookies. I went to the cash register to pay for it and saw a sign up on the wall that said: "Closed Tomorrow."

I asked the cashier, "Why are you closed tomorrow? What day is it, Sunday?"

He said, "No, no, we always close on Christmas Day."

I said, "You mean this is Christmas Eve?"

He said, "Yeah, didn't you know?"

Shaking my head, "No," I paid for the food. He put it in a bag and I left.

Without anybody seeing me I sneaked back into the building where I was staying, trudged upstairs, locked the door to the apartment, and slumped down near the steam until I got warm. Then I took off my coat and started to have my meagre Christmas Eve dinner—milk, bread, water and cookies. Afterwards, I put the milk near the window and opened the carton a little bit, so the milk would not spoil, and I could have some for tomorrow, Christmas Day. Then I went to sleep.

7
Squatter's Rights

---

*T*he next morning, I looked out the window. I had
a perfect view over Second Avenue and a view of
another church with a big, green, copper roof. I
could see glossy people streaming in and out of the
church, all dressed up, carrying boxes wrapped
with red and green Christmas paper, topped by glit-
tery ribbons and bows.

Hungry, I went to the window to get the container of milk I had put there. I discovered I'd
opened the window too much—the milk was frozen
solid; so I had to forget about it. But I broke off

some of the now stale, white bread, drank water and ate the cookies I had saved. I was thankful not to be dead or in a shelter.

As I sat there, I began to think about Christmases past, about my childhood, with all the new toys I would get on the holiday. Visions of the small, happy boy I had been, rose in my memory: blowing the whistle on my Lionel electric trains, running around the Christmas tree while my dog, Blackie, barked nonstop. In my mind's eye I saw Blackie running over to the whistle car (coal tender) behind the steam locomotive, picking it up in her mouth, knocking most of the trains off the track, then running under the bed with it and starting to chew it up. If I wanted to get the car back, I would have to get a piece of food, go under the bed, pet her and give her the food so she would let go.

My thoughts turned to my dog C.T., of whom I had just seen visions. I remembered a Christmas when he brushed by the tree and a glittering gold star fell off the top of the Christmas tree and hit him in the head. Angry, C.T. tried to bite the tree but instead bit into the extension cord that the Christmas tree lights were plugged into. He stood there, shocked, like a small child reprimanded. Yelping, he ran behind the sofa and hid for several days.

Looking at my scorched surroundings, I remembered my happy confusion in the past at this time of the year, because I did not know who to watch on television on New Year's Eve—Dick Clark or Guy Lombardo? I swallowed a bitter taste. Well, I did not have this problem anymore, since I had no television. Moreover, I had begun to wonder if my life would ever get back to what I had once considered normal again.

Christmas passed, then New Years. After that a period of time began when I lived my life in that room the same way the early settlers did. I had no electricity, running water, or gas for my stove. I would rise with the sun and go to sleep at sundown. I lost all track of time and didn't know what day of the week it was until Sundays, when the deli on Second Avenue was closed. Even then I hardly noticed.

After all, the time of day and day of the week were really irrelevant to me, because each day was just like every other. I spent them all looking out the window, sitting on a piece of foam rubber by the radiator. Outside, I saw only Second Avenue's litter or the other burned-out apartments. Inside, my thoughts were equally disheveled as I pondered what my fate was going to be. As time went on, my feet began to heal up, but somewhere along the line I twisted my left leg; in addition to the swelling, I developed water on the knee.

The poor diet I was eating had begun to take its toll on my body and mind. Lack of knowledge about nutrition, and very little money, forced me to depend on "killer combinations" of food. Once I found a letter in the kitchen and tried to read it. After twenty minutes, I figured out that the reason I couldn't was because the letter was written in Spanish. I began to think I might have had a small stroke, like my father before he had his major one. He too lost the ability to read. But in my case, I hadn't had a stroke. Lack of food, mental stimulation, and fresh air were taking their toll on me.

I didn't know how to correct the first two. However, the weather was getting warm, so I was able to open some of the windows, let some fresh air in, and not have to smell the pungent, burnt odor emanating from the two front bedrooms.

When spring came, the people living in the building who had been huddled in their apartments trying to keep warm all winter, began to stroll around the building, peering into the empty apartments, and spending time on the roof. Gradually, more people knew I was living where I shouldn't be. There were constant knocks on the door. But I knew better than to answer. The steel door on my apartment was very strong. When people banged on the door, they would hurt their hands, get disgusted, and leave.

One day, someone began banging really hard at my door and talked in Spanish, a mile a minute. Whoever it was stood outside the apartment for about an hour making a big, big racket.

When I peeked into the hallway from a hole in the bathroom wall, a Spanish man with a lot of kids and all kinds of luggage stood at my front door.

They were talking so loudly that someone who lived
in one of the apartments below me came running up
the stairs, calling in a gruff voice, "What the hell's
going on?"

Both men began speaking at a rapid pace; half
English, half Spanish. Apparently, the man with the
kids had sent a letter from Puerto Rico to the people
in this apartment to see if he and his family could
live here, and the family living here had said okay.
The man who lived downstairs gestured wildly,
"But that was before the fire."

"What fire?" asked the first man, wearily sitting
down on the collapsing suitcase beside one of his
children.

"There was a fire in this apartment and nobody
can live here now." I felt sorry for the people from
Puerto Rico, but I surely couldn't invite them in.
Looking at their tattered clothes I knew they must
be poor, and I wondered if they would find another
place to live, or would join the ranks of the homeless. Finally, they shuffled off.

A few days later I had to go out. One of the
disadvantages of this apartment was that when I
left, I could never lock the door behind me. Of
course, I knew there was nothing in it that anybody
would want to steal, so I was never that concerned.
However, that day, when I went out to get food and
returned, somebody else had taken up residence in
my apartment.

It was a female about forty or fifty. It was hard
to tell her exact age, because hardship had put so

many lines in her face and her brown-gray hair was stringy and unkempt. She was lying down on my foam rubber pad near the steam, making herself at home. I told her she had to leave, this was my apartment. But she really was "off the wall." She went flying around the apartment like a bat. I couldn't make heads or tails out of what she was saying. I was actually scared of her. I thought she might start hitting me. And if I hit her back, I would be in a lot of trouble, whether she was crazy or not.

I had to leave that apartment for a while. Luckily, this group of four interconnecting buildings had quite a few vacant, partially-burnt apartments that I could stay in until the crazy lady left my apartment. I kept checking.

One day, I saw her walking along in the street talking to herself. I mumbled, "Good, she's out of my apartment, so I can go back." The reason I liked the apartment she had been staying in was that it had a strong steel door. Most of the other burnt-out apartments had weak wooden doors. Also, I had accumulated a lot of things. Like televisions, air conditioners, and stereos. All kinds of broken appliances that I found in the burned apartments in this building. Someday, I planned, when I got my tools back, I would be able to fix and sell them.

My tools—it was time for me to go around to my old neighborhood to see the super. He was supposedly storing the tools I'd had to leave in the basement.

I walked over to my old neighborhood to see

him. He looked surprised, "Tools, what tools? I don't know anything about them."

I said, "Don't you remember? The marshal said you were going to hold them for me in the basement."

He replied, "I don't care what the marshal said, get lost." I should have known better than to believe anything a marshal says when he is evicting you. I had to forget about fixing up the apartment and the appliances I had in it. I could do nothing without tools.

Even though I had struck out with the super, I thought maybe I would have luck elsewhere. I remembered my friend John, the one who owned the pizza place, and the building it was in on 149th Street in the Bronx. He was the one I'd gone to see when I'd first found myself on the street. He had told me I might be able to have one of the apartments in his building. But it had to be fixed up first. And it would take a few weeks. It has been a lot longer than that. I decided to go back to see John.

When I found him, I said, "Hey John, remember that apartment, the one you were going to fix up, is it ready?"

He said, "Yeah, I fixed it. And I also rented it."

I said, "Oh."

He said, "Joe, I didn't know if you were going to come back." He paused, "Keep checking with me, maybe somebody will move out. Then we can work something out."

I said "Okay," and went back to my apartment.

Weeks passed. Then one day, I was sitting by the window looking out over Second Avenue, and I heard loud noises, coming from the roof. Looking up, I saw people staring and pointing at me. I couldn't understand what they were saying, but I could tell by the way they were acting that they did not like the idea of me living here.

Sooner or later, I knew, I would get kicked out of the apartment. I did not want to go back to living in the street. The only alternative left to me was to contact my father's side of the family.

My father's family was much larger than my mother's. I knew some of them were quite affluent, and would be able to help me.

The person I planned on seeing was my cousin Bill. He was the head of my family and a landlord. He owned quite a few buildings as well as the building he lived in, which was a converted mansion with ten apartments. A lot of my family were living there. Maybe I could stay with one of them, or in the basement. Or Bill just might have a superintendent job for me in one of the many buildings he owned. He would be able to help me—that is, *if he wanted to*. That was the question. That was something I would have to think about. Would it pay to spend the food money I made by selling scrap metal on a long distance phone call?

My cousin Bill was my Aunt Arlene's son. Arlene was my father's favorite sister. While my father was alive, she always seemed nice and congenial. I remembered how she used to make my father home-made macaroni. She had special feelings for my father—could any of those feelings be transferred to me? She was in her seventies now, and probably couldn't do anything for me. But her son Bill, could.

My mother's side of the family might have thought they had a reason not to help me, feeling I wasn't a good son. However, I was certain my father's side of the family could never say anything like that. I had done more than anybody could have expected for my father when he had his major stroke, and was in a coma for over a year before he passed away in 1968.

I remember how I found out about it. I was working. Late in the afternoon, I got a phone call from my Aunt Grace. I recognized her voice immediately.

She said, "Joseph, come home right away."

I said, "What's wrong?"

"Just come home right now!" she said in an agonized tone.

I told the foreman, "I got a personal problem. I gotta go home," and left. I rushed home and found my father lying on the sofa with all his clothes on. He looked like he was sleeping with his eyes open. I went over to him and bent down toward his face. I gave a sigh of relief; he was breathing. I began to call, "Dad, Dad please talk to me."

Later I found out he'd passed out, and fallen on

the floor in the living room early in the afternoon. Discovering him, my mother called our next door neighbor Pat, one of my father's elderly friends. He and my mother put my father on the sofa. My father must have already been in a coma at the time. My mother should have called the police or an ambulance immediately, but she kept thinking my father would wake up and be all right.

My father had been treated for his heart condition and his first stroke by a giant, private hospital in Manhattan. Arriving home I immediately called that hospital, then the police. The police responded quickly. They called an ambulance. Minutes later it arrived. They wanted to take my father to a city hospital. "No," I insisted, "all of his records are in a private hospital." The ambulance turned on its siren and red light as I got inside with my father. We sped off to the hospital. My mother and aunt followed in a cab. At the emergency room, the doctor on duty called one of the neurologists, and they admitted my father.

Hours later a tall, gangly resident came over to me and said sympathetically, "Well, look, with a stroke, it happens, it's done. Even if he was in the hospital as he was having it, there's nothing we could have done to help him. He's resting comfortably and his condition is stable. Go home, tomorrow will be time enough for you to see him."

I told my mother and aunt what the doctor had said, and we all decided to go home. When I got there, I called the hospital to inquire about my father's condition. They said "no change."

The next morning, before I went to work, I called the hospital again. Again they said "no change." I instructed my mother that if anything were to happen, "Call me *immediately* at the job." When she didn't, I breathed a sigh of relief.

After work I drove directly to the hospital to see my father. He was in the neurology department. In order to see how much brain damage was done they were working him up.

The doctor's report the next morning was grim. They said it was hopeless: he'd only live two or three days at best. I wanted to be at the hospital in case my father came out of his coma before he died and asked for me. The hospital staff was very compassionate, and let me stay all night. At intervals doctor and nurses would come in to keep me posted on my father's condition. Despite the doctor's prognosis, my father was very strong. He surprised the physicians and lasted about ten months. My mother and family would stay with him during the day. Then, after work, I would go directly to the hospital, and drive all of my family home. I'd go back to the hospital, and stay all night.

The care at the hospital was good. However, as the months passed by, he made no progress. I spent a lot of time talking to the doctors and nurses about my father; the medical knowledge I picked up would come in handy later on in life. After about eight months, one of the doctors said my father's condition was "chronic but not critical." In other words, he wouldn't expire at any minute. "There's nothing else we can do for him; it would be best for him to leave the hospital. Looking at my father, seeing his condition, I couldn't believe his words. "My father is bedridden. He can't walk, feed or wash himself, or talk. So he can't even ask for help. My mother will not be able to take care of him. He is too sick for us to take him home."

The doctor said, "No, no. I'm not saying you should take him home, but you need to check into arrangements to put him in a nursing home." He gave me a copy of my father's records to show the officials.

I made inquiries into nursing homes. The first thing their managers would say was, "We'd need a ten thousand or twenty thousand dollar donation." If I gave them the donation, they would put my father's name down on the preferred list. If I didn't, his name would be put down on a different, much longer list, and it would take about three years before he was accepted. Now although I worked hard, I didn't have twenty thousand dollars for a donation so my inquiries were to no avail.

As time went on, the words of the doctors at the hospital became more forceful, "We can't let your father stay here any longer."

I said, "You can't kick him out."

The doctor said, "No, we can't kick him out. But there's a mental institution we are going to put him in." Then they gave me its name.

I went to the mental institution to see what it looked like. It was a huge, beige, stone building located on an island. The only way to get there was to walk over a footbridge about a half a mile long. Inside, the atmosphere was disgusting. Inmates walked about aimlessly, visibly drugged, their eyes rolling about, saliva dripping from their open mouths. Some people lay on the floor in their own waste. Others called out gibberish or screamed until they were hoarse. The whole building was overcrowded and understaffed. Inmates were allowed visitors only a few days a week. Since the place was run by the city, they couldn't turn anybody down.

I was concerned about my mother. For her to see my father in a place like that would be enough to kill her. Her health was deteriorating. She could never walk over that long footbridge to see my father. Then there were my father's sisters. They were old and sick, and also could not walk over it. Although my father was not cognizant of his immediate surroundings, I was, and could not deal with the guilt I would feel. Despite the fact that my father remained in a coma, somehow I felt he recognized me, because he would never let the aides bathe him. He would fight them off with his still strong arms. But if I touched him, he would stop fighting and let himself be bathed. So, I knew he must still have some awareness of where he was. My father was a very strong and independent man his whole life. To place him in a mental institution if he was aware, and not able to walk out, would be the worst imaginable torture for him.

Meanwhile, I told the doctors, "No, I can't send my father there, find another place."

The doctors said, "You don't have any choice. This is a medical decision. If you can't find a nursing home that will accept him, we're going to have to move him there."

I made all kinds of legal threats. They fell on deaf ears. I still had hope that he would get better, but deep down, I knew that he wouldn't. Even so I didn't want his life to end in a mental institution. I made up my mind I was going to do whatever was necessary to make sure my father did not come out of the hospital unless he could go into a *good* nursing home where my mother and my family would know he was getting good care, and could see him frequently.

I consulted some of the best lawyers in New York. They all said that there was nothing that they could do. I thought, there's gotta be a way. If not with legal means, another way. That meant the "mob."

Now, I had been a legitimate, hardworking guy all of my life. I didn't know many underworld characters. But I knew a few. The place where I grew up and went to school was close to Pleasant Avenue in Manhattan. The mob was known to frequently hang around it. My idea was to somehow get a letter that looked like it was from the White House, asking the hospital to back off on the idea of moving my father.

At the library I found out what presidential stationery looked like and made copies of it. Then I was ready to see someone from the mob and ask if they knew somebody who could fix up a letter to look like it came from the White House.

I spoke to one of their numbers' guys. He gave me this advice. "You're a hard working guy. You're gonna be breaking Federal and State laws. They could lock you up twenty years later for doing something like this. Talk to our lawyer. He's the kinda guy, if you shot at a hundred cops in front of a hundred witnesses, he still could get you off. He's expensive like crazy. But we like people who take care of their families and for you there will be no charge."

At the lawyer's office I told him about my father, my family, and how bad the city mental institution looked. Then he told me, "The hospital is well within its rights. There is no law I can use to stop them. But there's a guy you should go see. He's an expert at laying down a smoke screen. We'll call him 'Smoke.' He'll tell you a way to do what you want without breaking the law."

I took his advice and saw Smoke. He told me how to confuse the hospital. And if they were confused, he said, they would do nothing. "Look, how is the hospital gonna know what presidential stationery looks like? I know a stationery store that will have everything you need. There's no reason to even try to attempt to go outside the law."

I went to the stationery store he recommended,

found some stationery that looked exactly like the ones I'd seen in the books, bought some and gave them to Smoke. He said, "Good, I will take care of everything, go home."

The lawyer also advised me to call on all my senators and congressmen, and ask them for help. He said they would love to write letters to the hospital on my behalf, to get my vote. "Start a barrage." I went to everybody I could think of. I don't know how many people I saw. Later, I found out from one of the hospital administrators that the director of the hospital got loads of mail. One letter, they thought, came from the White House.

The letters all said pretty much the same thing. They mentioned my father's name and recommended that care should be taken with his family. And they wanted to know the outcome—to make sure that my father and his family had been dealt with compassionately. One letter, that I saw, was from a congressman. He used words much better than I ever could. Some others were from business people. They were all good and very helpful. The letters placated the hospital administrators and they stopped bugging me about moving my father.

Moreover, the doctors began to take me more seriously. "You got a lot of political connections," they said.

I'd try to look nonchalant, "I know a few people."

I heard later that somewhere along the line, the

hospital got the idea I was mob connected, even though nothing was further from the truth.

Some of the doctors told other patients' families who were trying to get their loved ones into nursing homes that they should consult with me or ask for my help. A long line of people began waiting for me at the hospital day room every night. The day room became like my office at the hospital. They would tell me all the problems that nobody could help them with, like I was a godfather. Only I wasn't a godfather. I knew nothing, I was an ordinary working man.

My suspicions about the rumors about my mob connection were confirmed when a distinguished looking, salt-and-pepper-haired doctor from the hospital staff waited on line in the day room until after all the other people had left. Then he asked me for a favor. Trying to live up to my new image for my father's sake I said, "What is your problem?"

"There's a new landlord in my building that's bothering me."

I tried to look pensive, "Yes?"

"For the thirty years I've been practicing in my office in that building, I used to hold the outside door of the building open with a piece of cardboard during office hours, so my patients could walk right in my office. The new landlord said I can't do that anymore because it's a security risk. The wrong people can get in the building. Then they could break into the other apartments."

"This seems like a small thing," I murmured.

"Yes," the doctor nodded, "but it's hard for me to open the outside door with a buzzer when my patients ring the bell to get into my office. I can't answer the door while I'm examining somebody or taking their medical history because it disrupts my concentration."

In my most reassuring voice I told him I would see what I could do. Then I took his name, phone number and address and called up somebody I was very friendly with in high school. He now worked in the buildings department. He said he would see what he could do. Whatever my friend did turned out well, because two weeks later, the doctor came into my father's room, smiling, and told me the landlord had stopped complaining about the door.

That's when the rumors about me having mob connections really reached their pinnacle. I started to worry that somebody might "rub me out" by mistake, thinking I was trying to start a new mob, and take over. I went to my friend, the numbers' guy, and told him. He said he had heard stories about me masquerading as a Mafia kingpin, but I shouldn't worry about it, just deny it.

He also said in a half kidding, half serious voice, "If I know about it, the FBI knows about it. So don't do anything wrong, because they might be following you. And you'll get caught."

I swallowed hard, thanked him for the advice and left, determined to put the rumors to rest. But people were gathering around me more and more. They had all kinds of questions and favors to ask me. All I could do was give them common sense answers, because I had no mob connections. About two weeks later, my father got accepted into a "good" nursing home that had originally wanted a twenty-thousand dollar donation. I'm positive the doctor that I helped opened the doors for me.

A week after my father was admitted, I was in his new room when the chief administrator of the nursing home strode in, asking if he could speak to me. I murmured, "What now," and followed him. Once outside, I was shocked when he asked for two favors. One concerned a labor union that was causing the nursing home a lot of problems. And the other concerned the building department—some kind of violation the nursing home had. He'd tried lawyers and everything, and had gotten nowhere.

I was about to set him straight when I realized my reputation had probably gotten my father accepted; so I took down all the information. I thoughtfully replied, "Okay, I'll get back to you."

Again, I called my friend in the buildings department and asked him for help. In a few days my friend got back to me, and said that somebody had fouled up some paperwork at the buildings department. Everything was fine at the nursing home. All that had to be done was to have a secretary re-do some paperwork.

I went back to the head of the nursing home and told him that everything was straightened out with the buildings department. Then I gave him a common sense answer about the labor union. He didn't know how to thank me. He tried to give me money. But I said, "No, just see to it that my father gets the best care possible."

After that, my father got much better care than anybody else in the nursing home. They let me stay with him throughout the night, just in case he did wake up out of his coma and ask for me. I lived up to my responsibility one hundred percent.

My father's family couldn't have any gripes, because I did more than was expected of me. If my father's family refused me help, it wouldn't be because of anything I'd done.

The next morning I looked out the window. The Italian deli was closed, so I knew it must be Sunday. Then I saw people coming out of the church on 100th Street, with palm branches in their hands. So I knew this was Palm Sunday. Next Sunday would be Easter Sunday, which was always celebrated in my family with a big meal.

I thought "Am I going to be able to wrangle an invitation from my Aunt Arlene?" Like my mother's sister Lilli, Arlene had always given me invitations to come and eat and stay overnight with her on holidays, when I used to drive around in a sports car and dressed sharply. Aunt Arlene used to say she worried about me. Now that I had no money, no car, no sharp clothes, would she still be worried about me?

My father had always told me, "That's your

family. That's your flesh and that's your blood. They'll always help you out." I wondered if he was right. Or was he like me, an idealist and a dreamer? I was trying to evaluate the situation very carefully, trying to decide whether to spend my food money on a long distance phone call or not. I looked down at my body and skin. Because of the grime and my inability to wash regularly, my skin had weird looking goose bumps. My dirty clothes were rotting off my body, and were so stiff they were like cardboard. Pieces would fall off from my underwear as I walked. My brain was turning to jelly, I could not keep it clear. On the other hand, begging to my family sickened me. I had always been able to keep my head high.

Still I knew I could not go on this way. I had to get some clean water and good food. I hadn't had anything to eat or drink in two days. I had to call, and put my pride aside, hoping Aunt Arlene would let me have Easter dinner with her and her son Bill, and stay a few days or longer. I would soon have to leave this apartment. If I could not find a place to live, I would be back on the street where block associations would chase me until I dropped.

This, you might say, was the American version of the German-Japanese death marches of World War II. Where the Japanese would take the American prisoners, and the Germans would take the Jews from the concen-

tration camps, then put them in a forced
march to their death.

That's exactly what happens to the
homeless. They're forced and herded. Con-
stantly on their feet, with no food or water.
Or you might say it's almost like, the "Cru-
cifixion of Christ." But the homeless do not
carry a cross, they carry a shopping bag.

Gathering my courage I went outside to the
nearest telephone and called.

My aunt said, "Oh yeah. How ya been?" Very
polite and very nice. But try as I would, I couldn't
get an invitation to come and have Easter dinner
with her, or even find out whether I would be welcome in her house.

Finally I asked her, "Would I get kicked out if I
came up there?"

In an icy, but polite voice she said, *"Oh, we*
never kick anybody out."

Sighing, I knew that, in short, the answer was
no. She had been my last hope. I went back to the
apartment and wondered, "How long is it going to
be before I get kicked out?" During the next few
days I waited, knowing the end was near. People
came knocking on my door, but I would not answer.
They tried to break down the door; so they could
kick me out of the apartment. But the door was very
strong and nobody managed to break it in.

I stayed there till past Easter. Then two con-
tractors came in to the apartment next to me and

broke through the wall, took the steel door off the hinge and shouted in at me, "Get out of here, and if you come back, you'll find yourself floating face down in the river." Once again I was out in the street and could never go back.

At least, since it was spring, I no longer had the biting cold weather with which to contend. It was April. I had found a monkey wrench in a building, and was able to open fire hydrants, get some water, then scrounge up a little money for food by panhandling.

The days grew hotter. Summer came. One day I saw a fire hydrant, opened it, and washed my face and hands. Afterwards, I sat on the curb drinking some water out of a plastic cup I had. Two stocky cops walked over.

The older one said, "You opened this fire hydrant?" I couldn't lie. I had the wrench right there. He went on, "Look, there's a water shortage. It's against the law to open fire hydrants. Get out of this neighborhood, and don't open any more fire hydrants." The other cop grabbed my wrench. My access to water was gone. I had very little money. I was really in a jam. Food, I could do without, but water, I could not.

8

Water, Water Everywhere

Without the wrench, New York was like a barren wasteland. It was like being in the middle of the Mojave Desert. Even going to a restaurant and asking for a glass of water was no answer. If I walked in the door, they would take one look at me and say, "Get out."

I kept murmuring, "There has to be a place where I can find some water to drink and get cleaned up." The chemicals I had doused myself with, bug sprays, etc. really made me stink. I kept thinking, trying to find a solution. No answer came to mind, but I kept looking for one.

Finally, I remembered a park in Manhattan my mother used to take me to when I was a child. In earlier years, lots of horse-drawn carriages would come to the park. Outside, they had a special water fountain just for the horses. It looked like a bathtub with a special water faucet. When the horses pressed their noses against it, water spurted out.

One time when I was about six, my mother and I passed that fountain and I was thirsty. I stopped and tried to drink some water. My mother called out, "No, you can't drink that dirty water; horses drink out of there."

Now, remembering that place, I thought it might be the one spot where I could get some water. I headed over to this park, where I had spent some of my happiest childhood days and searched for that special water fountain. It was no longer there. Looking around, I remembered playing in the bushes nearby and finding a bird bath that had water in it. Climbing over the fence, I found the spot where the bird bath was. It was still there, but the water was not running. The only thing left for me to do was to go over to the playground where there were water fountains and a kiddy pool. Tired and thirsty from my long walk, I trudged there and sat down on a bench resting, looking at the kiddy pool and the whole playground. The sounds of my childhood, of playing there with my mother, my cousins, all the little friends that I had made in the park each summertime, echoed in my ears.

I looked at the small swings. They had special harnesses for very young children so they wouldn't fall out.

My mother and my Cousin Jill would swing me on them. I recalled sitting in my baby carriage watching Jill on the swings for older children. She used to stand up on the seat, then swing way up in the air, like she was going to swing all the way around the bar that held the chains. In those days, how wonderful she had seemed to me, and how I had longed to be old enough to do the same thing.

Turning to my left, I saw the monkey bars I used to climb. They had some kind of a crazy labyrinth with false entrances and exits. You had to figure out the right entrance to choose in order to come out the other end. How big they'd always seemed. Now looking at them, they seem to have shrunk. Time does a lot of strange things.

To my right was the sandbox I used to dig in. Once, Jimmy, one of my little friends, and I spaded up all sorts of loose change. We imagined we'd found a pirate's buried treasure. Excited, we kept on digging and digging. I don't know how far we went down—maybe three feet, then our dreams evaporated when we hit concrete.

My thoughts turned to Cass, another friend I used to come here with. Cass was older than me, nine to my five, but he was pale, very skinny, smaller and weaker than me. I always wondered why he wasn't bigger and stronger. Then one day my friend Cass didn't come to the park. I asked my mother what had happened to him. She quietly said, "Cass died. He had a blood disease." It was the first time death intruded into my happy world. How strange and alien it had seemed.

Twisting on the bench I focused my attention on the kiddy pool; looking at the nozzles on opposite sides of the pool shooting water about fifteen feet in the air. As I watched, rainbows formed on the water and a mist sailed through the air, cooling the whole playground. My eyes clouded. How much fun it used to be to play in the pool. How good it would feel, now, to wash myself with that nice cool water. I stared at the kiddy pool; memories flooding my mind.

When I got into my late teens and played in the Manhattan High School softball field, we all tried to hit the ball into that pool. It had to be a wide arc over the fence and tall fir trees. That was a real shot. Once you accomplished that, and word got around the neighborhood, your reputation was made. If you were a right-handed batter you were considered a right-handed pull-hitter. From that point on all the other teams would throw you fast balls on the outside corner of the plate, so you'd never be able to hit another softball into the kiddy pool.

If you wanted to stop them, you had to hit a ball in the opposite direction into the right field behind a fence onto the roof of Manhattan High School. Once you accomplished that, you were considered a real power hitter. Any time there was a money game around the neighborhood, people would come knocking on your door wanting you to play in it. Hitting a ball a great distance or into a difficult spot, like the hardball field, was very exciting. That field lay behind a fence and row of trees where there was some kind of automotive parts warehouse.

If you could hit a ball really good and it went on the roof of the automotive parts warehouse, all kinds of burglar alarms and security systems would go off. The place would light up like a pinball machine. Then a bunch of private detectives and security guards would come running out of the warehouse, with guard dogs sniffing and barking to see if somebody was trying to break in and steal anything. That was status: if you set off all the burglar alarms. You became an instant celebrity.

But eventually, the private detectives got wise to what was happening. One day, when we were playing in the hardball field, two muscled security guards from the warehouse strode over to us. The heavier one said, "Look, we don't want you guys setting off our burglar alarms anymore. Stop hitting balls on the roof of the warehouse."

Looking him right in the eye I said, "What are you, crazy? Who could hit a ball that far? And if you did hit a ball that far, who would be able to tell where it's going to go?"

The slimmer, taller guard replied, "Don't be cute, there's gonna be trouble. If anybody hits a ball on the roof again, and the alarms go off, we're gonna beat the shit out of all of you." They tried to scare us, but believe me, the only ones they scared were themselves. We totally disregarded their warning.

Now, the only time we were actually able to hit balls on the roof of the warehouse was in early spring or late fall. Because once the summer came, the fully blooming trees and thick foliage made it impossible to hit a ball over or through it. I remember one summer day when we were playing—must have been in July sometime—two security guards marched over with the usual threat that again they were going to beat us up if we hit any balls on the roof of the warehouse and set off the alarms.

As they spoke, my friend "Eu Botize" (that means crazy in Italian) came up to bat. The heavier guard grunted, menacing Eu Botize by brandishing his nightstick in one hand and banging it on his other hand. The gesture seemed to say, if you hit a ball on the roof of the warehouse I'm gonna bash your head open.

Turning, Eu Botize saw the guard. Baseball bat

124

in hand he ran toward the guard and started wildly
swinging at him. More security guards waited in
cars outside the park. The two inside radioed, calling other guards. They converged on the park, and a
fistfight broke out. Then some of the guys' girlfriends, who had been watching their boyfriends
play ball, got into the fight, scratching and biting the
security guards. Eventually, the city cops came,
stopped the fight and separated us from the guards.

Afterwards, the cops asked us, "What's going
on here?"

I said, "We didn't do anything wrong. It was
the security guards, they started the fight."

Then the cops went to talk to the security
guards, and came back to us. They said, "The security guards say you're setting off all the burglar
alarms in the warehouse."

I said, "Look, once in a while, somebody hits a
home run and the ball goes on the roof of the warehouse. And it accidentally sets off the alarms—I
mean, who can tell where a ball's gonna go? If you
hit a ball that far, who can actually direct a shot like
that?"

The city cop didn't buy it, "We're not gonna
arrest you, or give you any J.D. cards (juvenile de-
linquent), but we're gonna confiscate your baseball
bats."

I objected, "You can't take our baseball bats; if
you do that, we can't play baseball."

He said, "Good. You go find something else to
do. But leave these poor guys alone."

They took our baseball and softball bats. That meant no baseball or softball until we could get capital to buy more bats.

But being creative guys, we decided to play ball anyway. Not baseball or softball, but a game which had been invented for situations like the one in which we found ourselves—stick ball.

For stick ball all you need is a stick and a rubber ball. The stick would be a broom handle or mop handle that you could get from your mother, and if you were lucky enough to find a broken mop or broom in the backyard, you'd have a stick ball bat.

Next, we would have to find or create a rubber ball. We preferred Spaulding rubber balls, because they were best for stick ball. But many times, we didn't have enough money to buy one; so we used to do something called "sewer fishing." We knew the tides of the sewer system in our neighborhood. And if a rubber ball got lost in the sewer, even a long way off, it would generally wind up in a few choice sewers that we knew about. So we used to get a cardboard cup and a string, poke a hole through the lip of the cup, put the string through the hole and tie a knot in the string. We'd lower the cup into the sewers and fish out the rubber balls that were floating there. Then we'd scan all the labels and pick out a Spaulding.

Now, stick ball is a street game. To play it we painted bases in a few streets that didn't have too much traffic. During the game we made those Spaulding rubber balls curve and do crazy things by pitching them a certain way, and tried to see if we could hit a ball "two sewers" (that means the ball must sail over two manhole covers in the street). If you could do that, you were considered a pretty good hitter. We had fun, but no one really liked stick ball as much as softball. Moreover, people who lived in the blocks where we played stick ball often complained because we would obstruct traffic and cause other problems.

Two complaints I remember most vividly came from people who had stores in the block where we played stick ball. To one guy, we gave the name "Cyclops, the One-Eyed Monster," because we thought he resembled the monster in the movie, *The Odyssey*. "Cyclops" owned a jewelry store and always had a black plastic magnifying eye over one of his eyes, when he worked on a watch, or in the middle of his forehead, when he wanted to talk to somebody. It was held in place by a clasp on the back of his head. From time to time we hit foul balls into his store and knocked over the displays he had on his counter. Then he would come running out of his store, red-faced, and the black plastic eye in the middle of his forehead seemed to us to be glowing. We'd all point to him, laughing our heads off, calling "Cyclops."

Next to his store was a barber shop, and to the barber we gave the nickname "The Mad Doctor," after the doctor in the Superman comic books, who was always trying to kill Superman. Sometimes when we hit foul balls into his store, he was shaving one of his customers with a straight edge razor. A few times he cut his customers. As soon as that happened, he would run out of his store, the razor raised high in his hand, blood dripping onto his white uniform, and yell at us to stop playing ball. To us he was "The Mad Doctor."

Despite our wayward balls and bad jokes, it was "Cyclops" and "The Mad Doctor" who bought us new baseball equipment. They said they did it so we wouldn't bug them. We were all thrilled to be able to play again, because baseball really was our main thing.

Unfortunately, not long after that, Eu Botize almost caused a race riot. It happened when we were going to have a money baseball game with an all-black team from the West Side. We had played this team many times before and had always beaten them by ten or fifteen runs, but this was a summer of racial tension, not games.

Still, we wanted to play and so did they. After all, it was a money game. All of us expected the game to put money in our pockets. Usually, we played these games for twenty dollars a man. Every man on each team had to bring twenty dollars and show it to somebody else on the other team. For example, the opposing first basemen would show their money to each other, because it was your responsibility after the game either to pay your twenty dollars or to collect it.

These games usually took place on Sunday mornings around ten o'clock. This one was scheduled to be played in our park. That meant we were the home team, and would be the last at bat. We discussed the ground rules, got everything straight. Then our pitcher started to warm up. He looked good and was throwing hard.

The black team was first at bat. Our pitcher's fast ball was really "moving" ("moving" is baseball talk for a good fast ball that hops up or drops down, but always stays in the strike zone). They couldn't even get close to getting a solid hit off him; it was all pop-ups and weak ground balls. We patted each other on the back and whispered "Boy, we're gonna have twenty dollars in our pockets tonight for sure."

Then we got up to bat and noticed the black team had a new pitcher. As we watched, we gulped hard. This guy was unbelievable. He came from down South and had been brought in just for this game. His fast ball whizzed by each of our next batters before they could even get their bats up. We couldn't even get close to getting a hit off him.

I kept staring amazedly, my early hopes fading, as I mumbled dejectedly to myself, "Boy, this is gonna be one of those days."

The game went on and on. Now it was three up and three down. I groaned, there was a lot at stake, not only the twenty dollars, but there was our pride. We felt us Italians were the best the East Side had. Of course, we didn't consider the fact that the blacks thought they were the best the West Side had. There had been a lot of gang fights between blacks and whites that summer, to find out who was superior. And in our minds this game was somehow interconnected with the fights.

As the game's pitching frenzy continued, nobody was able to score on either side. The excitement grew. People started gathering around outside the fence, craning their necks, whispering and watching. Old Italian ladies came out of Mass, bought a cannoli (an Italian pastry) in one of the Italian bakeries in the neighborhood, and then stood behind the fence to watch their sons and friends play. Tension mounted.

We could see the women's white boxes tied up with a red and green string, full of Italian pastry, bounce up and down. Next to the women stood some Italian men who had picked up loaves of fresh Italian bread after church at one of the Italian bread stores in the neighborhood. The breads, wrapped in white paper, were under their arms. As they moved back and forth to see better the breads kept falling to the ground. Meanwhile some of the blacks' friends and families from the West Side arrived to see their team play.

The game was past its midpoint; nobody was scoring. Our winning was hardly the cinch we had planned on. Anytime someone hit a good ball, a great play was made and they were quickly tagged out. Around the fourth inning, some of our team members' girlfriends and their mothers came over to watch the game. That made us play even a little harder. We knew if we lost after all our bragging, the Italian women would never let us live it down. I heard it said one time that an Italian woman's mouth lives twenty years after her body dies and decomposes. It must be true, because they really know how to needle you.

Then, some of the old men who had been playing bocci (a game like horseshoes, but played with a ball) in the adjacent field stopped their game to come over to watch ours. Quite a crowd had gathered behind the fence looking at us. I looked up to see somebody very important and powerful arriving to watch us play.

His nickname was "Points," and it was said that he was a "godfather." As I watched wide-eyed, his bodyguard and chauffeur were opening the door of his Cadillac letting him out. I stared fascinated. He wore a white shirt with white embroidery on it. A tie hung around his neck. But it wasn't tied in a knot. The two ends were in a cross held together with a tie clip. And he had on blue, metallic-looking pants. As usual, his shoes were pointed—that's where he got his nickname "Points." The three men walked close to the fence and when they got to a spot he liked, "Points" opened up a small, collapsible chair and sat on it. His bodyguard held a beach umbrella over "Points" head, so no sun would get on him; and "Points" chauffeur had a small, battery-powered fan aimed directly at his employer, so he would be cool.

We were totally impressed, and sharpened our game even more. We tried hard to make something happen. But every time somebody hit a ball, and an out was made either at second or third base, the base runner would go sliding in with spikes up and knock over the second or third baseman. They would drop the ball and the runner would be safe.

The second and third basemen would protect themselves with the ball and the glove, using them like blackjacks. When they put a tag on you, they wouldn't just tag you once, they'd tag you two or three times. If you didn't slide in trying to get them, they would knock you off your feet with the ball and glove, and both you and the other guy would go down. Usually, you'd both get up with clenched fists. Combustion filled the air, but no one struck the match, threw a punch or gave in, in any way.

Well, it went on like that until the eighth inning. The tension was unbelievable. We knew something was going to happen but we didn't know what. Then a break came. One of our guys hit a long, low line drive to right field. The right fielder slipped in the outfield, and got a late jump on the ball. He came charging in. It looked for a while like he was gonna catch it, but then we saw he couldn't. Luck was going our way, because when the ball came down, it hit a rock in the outfield, then bounced off at a right angle to the right fielder, so he couldn't make a play on the ball.

The batter saw this, as he was rounding second base. He knew there was no score and it was probably going to be a one run game. He made up his mind he was going to score, and ran toward third base.

The right fielder couldn't make a play on the ball, so the first baseman rushed into right field to make the play. He got the ball, pivoted, and threw to home plate. The catcher was blocking the plate to stop the runner from scoring. The base runner went in, spikes up, dust flying, trying to knock the catcher over so he could not catch the ball to tag him out.

The ball and the base runner got to home plate about the same time. There was a roar of collision; then a cloud of dust. When the dust cleared, a fight had broken out. The catcher and the base runner were pounding each other with their fists.

We broke up the fight, but nobody knew yet whether the catcher actually caught the ball and put the tag on the base runner, or if he was safe and we were one run up.

Both teams and the umpires screamed and argued, but nobody could figure out what the true story was. Finally, the decision was that the base runner would go back to third base and it would be something that we called in those days "a do-over."

Now, there were two men out and no score. That meant we could score this run in one of three ways: a hit by us, an error by the opposing team, or a trick play.

The next guy up was Eu Botize. Eu Botize had a quick mouth and a good glove, but he couldn't swing the bat too well. We figured we'd better use a trick play to score the run. We decided to try a

133

squeeze play on the third pitch. Eu Botize was supposed to take the first two pitches (not swing at them). On the third pitch, he was to bunt the ball towards first base. Simultaneously, the base runner would run to home plate.

This is called a suicide squeeze play, because once it is started there is no way of stopping it. It was do or die. As Eu Botize swung, we prayed he could put the bat on the ball. Well, he did. As the runner slid home the catcher got spiked on his thigh from the collision. Blood spurted through his pants. There were no replacements, he had to continue or the blacks would have had to forfeit the game.

He got back down in his crouch behind home plate, wincing in pain. Now, Eu Botize, a real wiseguy, never could let an opportunity to come up with a wisecrack pass. He turned to the catcher, "Oh, did I step on your tail?" and he started to make noises and scratch under his arms like a chimpanzee.

The catcher went crazy. He got up out of his crouch, grabbed Eu Botize around the neck, and started to strangle him. Now the catcher was a huge guy, well over six feet and had arms that looked like tree trunks. Eu Botize was very slight; he was around five feet and very skinny. The scene looked like some of the old monster movies where Frankenstein crushed his foe like a cardboard box. Swinging wildly, Eu Botize tried to punch the catcher, but his arms were too short. The catcher put one hand on top of Eu Botize's head like he was a puppet and laughed uproariously.

When this happened, a full-fledged fist fight broke out between the teams. It wasn't really the incident we were fighting about, it was superiority, racial pride. In our minds it was all gonna be straightened out either in the ball game or in the fight.

Some of the old men, the bocci players, and even an old lady, a widow, all dressed in black, screamed, "Stop the fight!"

Suddenly, "Points," the godfather, stood up and yelled at his bodyguard and chauffeur, "Stop it. I mean now."

That did it. Everyone quieted down for the minute, but I knew there was a good chance this incident would trigger more race riots and gang fights. The fighting had reached a high point a few months before this ball game.

One of the gang members from the West Side, who was really good with his hands and knew no fear, had decided he didn't care about the rules of the street. He was going to tread on some of the East Siders' turf and go into one of the East Siders' sanctuaries—the park that the kiddy pool was in.

He ran into a few East Side gang members, resulting in his own death. His head was bashed open with bench slats (bench slats are the wooden planks, approximately two by four inches by four feet long, that are bolted to the metal portions of park

benches. If you knew how, you could break loose
the bench slats and use them as bats). They hung the
West Sider upside down from one of the trees in the
park "with his brains hanging out of his head." It
made the newspapers and filled the streets with
cops—twenty-four hours a day. Even so, it was a
long, long time before the fighting finally stopped.

Now it looked like it was going to start again.
The godfather called his bodyguard over and whispered something to him. The bodyguard strode over
to us and said in a loud voice, "Stay right here.
Don't move and keep your mouths shut." We
watched wide-eyed as the bodyguard made a phone
call from a nearby candy store. He came back and
announced to everybody who had come to watch,
"The game's over. Go home." Everybody left, except
a couple of guys' girlfriends. When the bodyguard
looked at them menacingly, they left too. We were
all thinking, "What is going to happen now? What
kind of a jam are we in? Just how angry is the godfather?"

We didn't dare ask. We waited and waited. No
one uttered a word. About an hour later an open
garbage truck showed up and stopped outside the
baseball field. The bodyguard walked over to us and
ordered, "Get in." Without protest both teams
obeyed. "Now," he said, "Keep your mouths shut."
Again we obeyed, still silent, our eyes riveted on
him.

Then the godfather, his bodyguard and chauffeur got into the limousine and it started up Second

Avenue. We followed them in the garbage truck. About a half hour later, we pulled up outside an Italian restaurant in Brooklyn. The bodyguard got out of the car and tapped on the door of the restaurant. When it opened, he motioned to all of us to come in. We piled out of the truck and quietly walked into the restaurant.

After we got inside, the owner, who stood at the door waiting for the godfather to come in, locked the door behind us. The godfather scrutinized us. We couldn't tell whether he was smiling or frowning. A few seconds later, he disappeared into a room behind a curtain, followed by his bodyguard and driver.

Shortly after that, the bodyguard sauntered back to us and said, "Sit down," then he pulled a bunch of tables and chairs together.

We did as we were told, sitting around the tables. The owner walked over to us and said, "Pick out any food you want on the menu. It will be free."

A hand from behind the curtain waved the bodyguard to return. The bodyguard went into the room and came back out, this time with a fist full of money.

He handed each one of us a twenty dollar bill and said, "Everybody won today. Nobody lost. Everybody is a winner. Eat your food and enjoy."

Then the bodyguard went back to the room where the godfather was. Music began pouring out of a high fidelity system. It was Caruso singing Pagliacci.

The food arrived, steaks, chops, lasagna, and spaghetti—a veritable banquet. Hungry, we began eating. We were just starting to talk and enjoy ourselves when "Points," the godfather, came out of the room and walked over to Eu Botize.

He called Eu by his correct first and last name. Then he walked over to the black catcher and called him by his correct first and last name and said, "Shake hands. There are going to be no fights. It was a good game and everybody will stay friends." No one spoke.

He smiled a tight-lipped smile, "Do you understand?" He stared first at Eu Botize, because "Points" knew Eu Botize was a wise guy. Then he called everybody on each team by their correct first names and last names and said again, "There are gonna be no fights. It's over. Understand? *Capice?* Don't make me mad." Then he smiled again and went back to the room behind the curtain, saying, "And now for dessert."

Dessert was spumoni (Italian ice cream), black coffee, and pastry. And some special entertainment —two strippers, one black and one white.

We turned toward the pool table in back of the restaurant that would be the girls' stage. The white stripper got up on the pool table. The lights dimmed, a spotlight shone on her. Her scanty costume was composed of a white and gold bra and panties studded with sequins and rhinestones, plus cowboy boots. A cowboy hat was perched on her head. Beneath it, long blonde hair hung down to her waist.

As she stepped forward they shut off Caruso and put on disco-type music. We watched, our eyes widening as she began a provocative dance. After she finished, the black girl got up and moved into the spotlight. She had on a red cap, bra, panties, fishnet stockings, a garter belt, and high-heel spiked shoes. As we watched her beautiful body moving, we all started to get excited.

Each girl would take a turn dancing fifteen minutes. This went on for about an hour. By the end of the hour, neither girl had any clothes on whatsoever except for their hats, and their dancing had progressed from suggestive to wild.

Then they started to talk and tell jokes. The white girl had finished her most provocative dance so far, and was telling jokes and stories about her sexual exploits with her boyfriend. According to her, "One night we were watching the ball game on TV. My boyfriend was so passionate, he would kiss me in between the strikes. And to return his passion I would kiss him between the balls." Well, that was the finale of her act.

Then the black girl got up to do her final dance. It was very sexual, very explicit. She began telling jokes about her exploits with her boyfriend. She called the waiter and said, "Let me have a beer stein, a whiskey glass, a half a dollar, and a piece of gum." The waiter gave her what she asked for.

First she took the gum and started chewing it. Meanwhile, she put the beer stein face down on top of the pool table. Then she took the whiskey glass, turned it upside down and put it on top of the beer stein. Taking the gum out of her mouth, she stuck it on the upturned bottom of the whiskey glass. Afterward, she took the fifty-cent piece and stood it up in the gum so that it would stand up on edge. Smiling she started to dance finally squatting over the whiskey glass where the half-dollar was standing. She picked it up with her snatch. That was the finale of her act.

The lights came on. Both girls walked to the back of the restaurant into two separate rooms where there were card tables, sofas, and chairs. We were told that if anybody on either team desired either one of the girls, he could go in one of the rooms and enjoy himself.

One of our team members, we used to call him "Howdy Doody"—because his freckled face looked like the puppet Howdy Doody in the children's show—got up and started to walk toward one of the rooms. I said, "Howdy Doody, you're not going over there, are you? What are you, crazy?"

He said, "Look, these girls are clean. They've got no needle marks on them. No nothing. They're not junkies. They won't let anybody in here with anything."

I said, "Hold on. Those people don't have no crystal balls. Those girls are working girls and this is Sunday. They've been working all night, Saturday."

He said, "I'm sure they're okay."

I asked, "Do you remember the last girl you thought for sure was okay? The farmer's daughter from Indiana?" He looked at me and started to think. Then I said, "Don't think too much. I'll remind you."

"This is what happened. One Saturday night around 2 a.m., you and I were riding around in your brother's car and found this beautiful girl walking in the street in midtown Manhattan. She was the proverbial farmer's daughter from Indiana. One thing led to another and she got in the car with us and we talked until nearly four in the morning. She said she felt passionate that night, but she didn't want to do anything in the car. Since it was summertime, we decided we'd go to Orchard Beach, even though the beach was closed at this time of night. Dawn was breaking. Everything was closed, but you drove the car over the grass and other embankments onto the sand on the beach.

"We all got out of the car, looked around to see where there would be some privacy, then found a wooded area with some grass and weeds where, if you were lying down, nobody could see you. We took turns going in there with the beautiful farmer's daughter from Indiana.

"By the time she finished with us it was daylight and she had all her clothes off and felt like dancing on the beach nude. Fishermen passed us in their boats, looking at her. They couldn't believe their eyes. She was very beautiful and well built. Then the fishermen started beaching their boats, and began to come up on the beach towards us.

"We figured we'd better get out of there quick. We all got in the car and tried to drive off the beach. Only the car was stuck in the sand; so we had to get out of it and rock the car as the girl drove it off the sand and onto the grass. It was a miracle that we were able to get off that beach. We drove as fast as we could back to midtown Manhattan, brought the girl to her hotel, got her phone number, and went home.

"The next day everything was fine. But the day after, we both started to burn when we urinated. Each of us went to his own doctor and told them the story about the girl. Both doctors took blood tests and cultures and asked if we had any discharge? We both answered, 'No.'

"The doctors said the same thing. 'Looks like VD. Call up the girl and tell her to come and see me or her doctor.' They started us on antibiotics and we were told that the infection should be gone in a day or so. But after several days there was no improvement.

"We went back to my doctor and tried to call up the girl, but she had been kicked out of her hotel room for having wild parties. 'The bad news,' the doctor said, 'is we can't check her. The good news is that the test results were negative.' The doctor took more blood tests and cultures. Then he said, 'Maybe you've got something that isn't susceptible to the antibiotics you were given. Let's try a different one.'

"Again he suggested we come back in a couple of days. After they passed and we were still burning like crazy when we urinated, we headed back to our separate doctors. Neither knew what to make of it, so they had to report our problem to the Board of Health. The Board of Health came to our homes to see if we were giving what we had to our parents, or anyone who lived with us, and to take more cultures. Of course, they told our parents what had happened. Our parents yelled and screamed.

"This went on for almost a month. Our parents cursed. We grew more scared. We didn't know what we had. We thought they might end up cutting our penises off if it didn't get better.

"After a month of our thinking we might die or worse, the doctors hazarded a guess as to what might have happened: When we were making love in the bushes there might have been some kind of a pesticide on the grass, and somehow we got it on ourselves and got an irritation which caused the infection. They gave us an antibiotic salve with cortisone. Finally, that cleared up the problem.

"So," I said, "Howdy, you thought that girl was okay, too. And we never really knew whether it was the girl or the grass or what, because the doctors could never check the girl. And I'm sure in a few days nobody will be able to find these girls, either, if something is wrong. The doctors won't be able to check them. Our old trouble could be nothing compared to the new trouble you'll be letting yourself in for now."

Another team member was standing next to us. His nickname was "Shovel Feet" (because when he walked, his big feet looked like shovels). Shovel Feet told Howdy Doody—"You know, Howdy, it won't be a smart thing for you to go in with one of those girls."

Howdy Doody told Shovel Feet, "Look—when it comes to smarts, you ain't got none. Remember 42nd Street?"

Howdy Doody was talking about an incident at a disco bar we used to go to. At the bar there was one particular girl dancer with long black hair and green eyes, who was very beautiful. Shovel Feet wanted to take her home one night, but she said, "My boyfriend is going to pick me up later." Shovel Feet didn't take her word. He wanted to take that girl home in the worst way. At midnight, the girl's boyfriend, a big strong guy from Little Italy, showed up. Shovel Feet decided he was going to get rid of him.

First, he tried talking rough to the boyfriend

and scaring him. The boyfriend stared for a minute at Shovel Feet, then passed it off, laughing. This made Shovel Feet more determined. "Look," Shovel Feet said to him, "Let's go outside and straighten it out."

They went outside. Now this is at 42nd Street, Broadway area, two o'clock in the morning. Shovel Feet grabs the girl's boyfriend around the neck, forces him to the ground, then shoves a gun in his mouth and orders him to leave.

The boyfriend's buddies from Mott street and the guys from our neighborhood began to gather around them, each cheering their friend on and shouting insults at his opponent. In minutes they were jabbing and punching. A full-scale fight broke out. It was broken up fast by the bouncers. Some of our neighborhood guys grabbed Shovel Feet and said, "Look, there's a lot of people here. For sure somebody called the cops. You'd better get out of here." Shovel Feet left, and the girl's boyfriend, who must have gotten the same advice from his friends, also left.

The outcome was that Howdy Doody took that girl home.

Remembering all that, Howdy turned to Shovel Feet and said, "Look, when it comes to smarts, you ain't got none. So I'm gonna do what I want."

Howdy got in line, waiting to go into one of the

rooms. Then Shovel Feet asked him, "Aren't you going to get some whipped cream?"

The reason he asked that was because Howdy Doody liked to use whipped cream to sweeten his sexual encounters, and we all knew it because the cops in the neighborhood told us an especially funny story.

One winter night, Howdy Doody was parked off the East River Drive in a dead-end street with a girl. Both of them were sitting in one of the bucket seats. The cops were on patrol, passed this car, and saw that the windows were all fogged up. They could see only one head. It was moving back and forth. They thought someone was having a heart attack or dying.

So they stopped their squad car, got out, and went over to the passenger side of Howdy Doody's car. When they opened up the door, Howdy Doody fell out, a can of whipped cream in his hand. The girl sat there immobilized, her dress all the way up in the air. The cops looked at Howdy Doody—"Your head shouldn't be down there."

Later, the cops told people around the neighborhood about the incident. That's how Howdy Doody got his reputation. And the only thing Howdy Doody would say about it was that he liked whipped cream.

* * *

Howdy Doody waved as he reached the door. Later on, he came over to me, flourishing the red garter belt and stockings the black girl had given him. And he was very happy. In later years, Howdy Doody would joke that the red garter belt and stockings the girl gave him that night kept him out of the Army.

That story happened when we still had the draft and everybody had to go down to an army office for a physical to be classified. Army doctors were not too fussy. If you could walk, you would wind up in the Army—regardless of what you told them was wrong with you.

Well, Howdy didn't want any part of the Army. The day he had to go for his physical at Whitehall Street, he wore that girl's red garter belt and stockings, makeup, and a sanitary belt and napkin. When he got to Whitehall Street he was acting very effeminate. Then he was questioned about why he had on a sanitary belt and napkin. Howdy said that he liked to be safe and didn't like a mess. Now, there's part of the physical when a doctor asks you to bend over and looks up your poop. When the doctor told Howdy Doody to bend over, Howdy told him, "You're cute," and "Don't be fresh."

Well, the act worked. The Army doctors thought he was gay. Everybody that was standing on line with him began making fun of him and calling him a faggot. But inside, he was laughing at them, saying to himself, "I'm going to be home, enjoying myself, playing with their girlfriends, while they're being tough guys in the Army." He told this story many, many times and kept laughing about it.

Howdy Doody was really a pretty sharp guy. He managed to do what a battery of lawyers couldn't have done—Make himself 4-F.

9

Faith, Love, and Charity

---

*I*t was time to stop resting and remembering; I planned to wade into the kiddy pool to get cleaned up. Taking off my shirt, shoes, and socks, I put them in my shopping bag, thinking how good it would feel to get into the water and wash my aching body and feet. Afterwards, I would drink some cool, clear water from the fountain. I started to walk toward the kiddy pool.

A police car pulled up outside the playground. Two cops jumped out, came into the playground, and walked toward me. They stood between me and the kiddy pool, motioning to me with their night sticks, shouting, "Hey, hey, hold on, hold on."

I waited for them to come over. When they got close the big-boned, ruddy-complexioned one said, "What are you going to do?"

I replied, "Wash up a little, then have some water to drink from the water fountain."

The cops scrutinized me and the dark, smaller one drew together his beetle brows: "Look, this is a kiddy pool, it is only for kids. This is no bathhouse or flop house."

I said, "This is a public park and there's water in the pool. Is there any reason why I can't go in there and wash up?"

The taller one raised his nightstick, "Look, get out of here while you can still walk. Just get out of here. And don't ever let us catch you here again. Leave while you can still walk."

I said to myself, "Where do I go from here?" Then I thought of something I hadn't tried—find a play street that had a fire hydrant with a sprinkler cap.

I found one. Children in their brightly colored bathing suits were playing in the water with plastic water toys. But it was the same as the park—somebody called the cops and I had to leave.

I kept on walking for days with no food or water, until I just could not walk any more. I ended up at 110th Street, off Lexington Avenue, in front of a scorched, sealed-up building. Exhausted, I sat down, my back against the stone-cold grafitti-strewn wall of the building.

When I saw the bar, restaurant, and grocery store on Lexington Avenue close, I knew it was late at night. And there would be nobody in the street to tell me to leave or bother me. So, lying down I went to sleep.

Just before daybreak, I was wakened by a stinging pain in my leg and back. I pulled my pants leg up to see what was causing the pain. A water bug was biting me and more were crawling on me. Jumping up on my feet, I took off my clothes, shook them out—more water bugs fell out.

I had to forget about sleep for the rest of that night. Putting my clothes back on, I sat and waited for dawn.

As streaks of light filtered into the dark sky, the neighborhood started to come to life. First came a bakery truck, delivering bread and rolls to the restaurant and the grocery store that was still closed. The truck driver had a key to the restaurant's steel gate. He opened the gate and put a big bag of fresh bread and rolls behind the gate. I could almost smell the pastry aroma. Then he went to the ice machine outside the grocery, opened a lock on the chain around the ice machine that held the door closed, put a bag of fresh bread and rolls in the ice machine, put the chain back across the door and locked it, then left in his truck.

As daylight spread, a stream of rats raced out of the garbage cans with pieces of food in their

151

mouths, heading, I guessed, back to their homes in the sewers and down cellar steps.

Gradually, the stores started to open up, the lemon-faced sun came out, and I could see people walking down Lexington Avenue to the subway stations to go to work. Then I thought of a friend who worked close by. His name was Stan.

Stan owned a car parking garage in Manhattan. I thought I would go there because garages have water they use to wash cars. Maybe Stan would let me wash up—or even better—stay in one of the wrecks he had stored there until he could work on it.

It was still too early to see him. I had to kill time 'til he came. I walked to a big white church that covered one square block a few blocks from the garage. I was lying in the street near the church, out of the sun, and some guy passed me by, "Hey, you know, you can get some free food."

I asked, "Who gives out free food?"

He answered, "They give it out in the church."

I said, "Where do I go?"

He said, "Go right in that door and ask them for some food," he pointed.

I responded, "Great," got up and went into the church. There was only one office open. Inside was a gray-haired, dowdy woman in a brown uniform (she was some kind of a sister).

I asked her, "Do you give out free food here?" Right on the desk in front of me was a bunch of sandwiches wrapped in cellophane.

She said, "Look, we don't give out food out of *that* door."

"I'm pretty tired, and pretty sick," I said slowly. "I really can't walk that well."

She gave me a distasteful look, "See here, I'm not even going to even talk to you unless you come through the other door."

"What other door?" I said wearily.

She said, "You have to go around the block and come in the door that says 'Food.' Then I'll talk to you."

I walked out into the street again. I was so weak, it took me three quarters of an hour to walk around the whole block to the door with the sign that said "Food." I walked into the same office, through a different door. "Can I have some food?" I asked.

Seeing me again she pursed her lips, "Well, look, we can only give you food if we have any left over, after the children eat. This food is mainly for the children."

I said, "You made me walk all around the block just to tell me that?"

She said, "Look, that's procedure."

Well, I really went crazy. "Who the hell do you think you are?" I said, my voice rising in anger and humiliation. "How can anybody be that indifferent and rotten?" I walked out and sat down in the street by a car. I was really fuming, and feeling weaker and sicker every minute. Then one of the workers, who was in the church when I was talking to the sister, brought me out a cheese sandwich that he had hidden under his shirt. As I grasped it, and pushed it into my mouth, my hand trembling, he just looked at me and shook his head.

Afterward, pulling myself together, I made my way back to Stan's garage and found him. "Look, I need a place to stay and I have to get something to eat and drink. Could I use some of the water you have around here, maybe sleep in one of the wrecks you keep in the back before you take them into the body shop upstairs?"

He asked, "What happened to you, Joe? You look terrible."

I answered, "Things are bad right now. I got evicted from my apartment and I need a place to stay. I have to get off my feet and rest."

Then he said, "Look, there is a van in the back of the garage that we're going to take to the body shop in a week, week and a half. You can sleep there for a while. You're welcome to any of the water we've got here. And here's a couple of bucks so you can buy some food."

I said, "Thanks."

Stan said, "You can't make this your permanent house, but for a couple of days, a week, fine. Later, when I get time, we can sit down and talk. Maybe I can help you out with some advice."

I nodded, "Okay."

Taking some of the money he gave me, I went out to a grocery store, bought some food, came back to the garage and went to find the wreck in which

Stan said I could stay. I had ate a little something, then washed up a bit and started to feel better.

The garage closed at midnight and stayed closed until eight o'clock the next morning. I breathed a sigh of relief. For the first time in weeks I would have peace, quiet, and security. Nobody would throw me out. I could sleep soundly through the night.

The night watchman walked over, "If you want to go out and get something to eat, do it now. I'm about to close." He waited for me to come back. Next to the wreck in which I would be sleeping they'd parked six or seven hearses. It seemed appropriate. I wasn't that far from death myself.

I didn't wake up until around seven the next morning when they opened the garage and started to move cars around. Then I walked over to the water faucets over a big oil drum. With a "squeegee" (that's two rollers with a hand crank that's used to wring out wet towels after they're used to wash cars), I washed my face and hands. People came to pick up their cars; they looked at me questioningly but said nothing.

Suddenly, I was startled by the appearance of someone who was my enemy—the sister from the church up the street. It turned out that she parked her car in the garage, and she was a leader in this neighborhood. When she spotted me, she rushed over to Stan who was getting ready to pull a car into the garage and really laid into him. I looked at his face. It was all red, but he could not tell her off. I kept listening, as she chewed him out. When she finished and left, he raced outside as if he wanted to cool down from having to keep his mouth shut.

He came over to me and sighed, "Joe, you can't stay here anymore. Believe me, I'll get into a lot of trouble with my customers, especially with that woman. She could cause me a lot of problems around this neighborhood."

I said, "I can understand that, Stan. I don't want to cause you trouble."

His eyes were bleak, "I don't want to send you back out on the street. Is there any way I can help you?"

I said, "Well, could you get me to my family in Suffern County?"

He said, "I can't take you all the way up there myself, but I can make arrangements for you to get there."

I nodded, "Good."

Then he said, "These people are Italians, right? They have to help you, you're their flesh and blood."

I inclined my head thoughtfully, "Yes, I hope they do."

He looked me in the eyes, "Do they have any reason not to help you?"

"No," I said quietly.

He said, "Okay, then I'll make the arrangements."

He spoke to Hal, a young Hispanic gypsy cab driver who parked his cab in the garage, and asked him to take me to my family. Then he gave me twenty bucks and wished me luck. He said, "If you miss connections with your family or something, come back. But make sure nobody sees you."

I shook his hand, "Thanks."

Climbing into the back of the gypsy cab, I made myself comfortable for the long ride to Suffern County to see my cousin Bill and Aunt Arlene, "my father's favorite." The same person who said, *"We never throw anybody out."*

When the cab pulled up in my cousin's driveway, I saw my family sitting in the backyard having sugar cookies and iced tea. When they saw the gypsy cab pull up, my cousin Bill (who is the spokesman for my family) and his mother, Arlene, got up, walked over to the cab, looked in the back seat and saw me.

His voice was icy as he asked, "What are you doing here?"

I said, "I need help, I need a place to stay, and some food. I've got nowhere to go. My parents are dead. I'm all by myself, you know that."

Aunt Arlene shook her head, "Well, there's really no place for you to stay here."

I stared at her, "This is a big house, a converted mansion. You don't have a spare room? Or maybe you can let me stay in the basement, you people always used to invite me to stay here."

She said, "That was then, this is now. It's different."

My face fell, "All I want is a couple days of decent food and a place to sleep."

Bill said, "Look, you might have some kind of disease. Something may be wrong with you. Go back to New York, put yourself in a hospital, get yourself cleaned up. The family will stand behind you one hundred percent when you get out of the hospital, I give you the family's word. But right now, there's something wrong with you. We're not doctors and there are no hospitals around here. Go back to New York."

I began to plead, "Just give me something to eat," and I opened the door starting to get out of the cab.

But Bill slammed the door shut and said, "No, go back to New York."

Embarrassed, I turned to Hal, the gypsy cab driver, "Look, you have to take me back to New York."

He looked at me sympathetically, "Well, you can't go over to the garage no more."

I nodded, "Yeah, I know."

He said, "Anywhere else I can take you?"

I sighed, "Yeah. A friend of mine named Ellis owns an ice cream company in the Bronx, on Minad Street, near Hunts Point Market. Do you know where that is?"

Hal shook his head, "I know where Hunts Point Market is, but not Minad Street."

I replied, "You get to Hunts Point. I'll tell you how to get to Minad Street."

About two hours later, we pulled up outside my friend's ice cream company. I thanked the cab driver, got out, and asked one of Ellis' workers for him.

He said, "Ellis isn't here now but he'll be back later." I told Hal that he could go and I'd wait for my friend.

Hal said, "Take care of yourself." And, in a change of roles I would have found funny at any other time, he gave me some money and left.

As I was walking towards the open garage door, the foreman Steve, whom I knew, sauntered up and asked, "Joe, what are you doing here?"

I said, "I want to see Ellis and see if he'll give me some help." He looked me up and down but didn't comment on my threadbare clothes.

"Well, Ellis isn't here, but you're welcome to stay. Come inside and sit down."

I said, "I'd rather sit outside in the fresh air till you finish moving the trucks around."

"O.K." Steve answered quietly, and gave me a milk box to sit on. I sat down in the shade, feeling the breeze from the Bronx River.

He smiled, obviously trying to be helpful, "Hey, you want some ice cream? We've got tons."

I said, "Not right now, maybe a little later."

I sat there quietly, pensively, trying to relax. Suddenly I saw smoke coming from across the street. Yelps and screams came from the smoke. I couldn't understand what was going on. My mind was already confused, and this confused it even more. Yelps and screams coming from a cloud of smoke? What in the world was going on? I walked over there to investigate and felt nauseated. A bunch of kids had found a sick, lame dog and were putting cigarette lighter fluid on him. Then they set the dog on fire by throwing lighted matches on him. Horrified, I watched the dog running in circles to escape the pain. Grabbing him, I smothered the fire with my shopping bag, and began yelling at those kids. I wanted to scare them badly, so they wouldn't turn around and try to set me on fire too.

After they ran away, I walked back toward the dog and covered the burns on his body with a piece of newspaper I picked out of a nearby garbage can. Softly talking to him, I tried to comfort him.

Now this dog could have almost been a twin of my old dog, C.T. The only difference was my dog had one white paw, and a blemish on the side of his face that this dog didn't have. Their coloring and size were almost identical. Looking at it, I wanted to believe that this was my dog, but I knew it wasn't. As I talked to him I started to pat him on the head. He opened his eyes and I shuddered. His eyes were pure red. I don't mean the whites of his eyes were bloodshot or cloudy—there were no whites in his eyes—only red. You could not see his pupils. This dog was really sick.

I certainly didn't know how to treat him, but since I hadn't been able to help C.T. I could at least help this animal. I went over to my friend's ice cream company and asked to use the phone. The watchman said, "Sure, go ahead."

I called the Animal Medical Center in Manhat-

tan and said, "I have this sick dog that can't walk.
Do you have an ambulance?"

The woman who answered replied, "No, but
there are private animal ambulances you can call."
She gave me a phone number to try.

Now, the procedure is that you call them and
they call you back when an ambulance is available
to pick up your pet. I called the ambulance service,
and waited for them to call me back. I knew I could
pay for the pick-up with the money Stan and the cab
driver gave me, so I would be able to get this dog
some treatment.

Since I had to wait for the call, I sat back down
to catch my breath. All of a sudden a man strode to
my side of the street and walked up to the dog. I
said, "Is that your dog?"

He said, "Yeah, I've been looking for this dog
for about three weeks. I didn't know what happened
to him 'til one of my friends came in my store and
told me some kids were setting a dog that looked
like mine on fire." He continued, "I'm going to take
care of him. I'll make sure he gets to a vet." A couple of minutes later somebody else came with a
piece of plywood. The men loaded the dog onto it
and took it away.

I felt better. At least that dog was going to get
taken care of. I called the ambulance service, and
told them they didn't have to come. Then I sat down
on the box to wait for my friend Ellis.

Maybe half an hour later, a group of people
marched up the block. There were about twenty-five

men. Behind them walked the kids who'd been setting the dog on fire, followed by three or four
women walking behind them, egging them on, saying things like, "Get rid of him, kill him." One guy
had a rifle case, and the other men carried all kinds
of weapons like baseball bats, tire irons, pipes, etc.

At first, I looked around to see who they were
talking about. Then they came walking over to me
and I knew. One said, "You bothering these kids?"

I shook my head, "No, I ain't bothering no
kids."

The women called out, "Hit him. Beat him up.
Kill him. Get him out of here." Their faces were red
and grim. They looked like they were ready to kill
me.

The spokesperson said, "Our sons said you
were bothering them."

I said, "Your sons were setting a dog on fire."

The guy with the rifle case walked closer. "My
sons don't do things like that," he bent his angry
face toward mine. I got to my feet figuring I'd better
defend myself any way I could, but knowing I was
about to get my head handed to me.

Just at that moment, a lean, tall guy got out of a
car parked nearby. He walked over, stationing himself between the crowd and me. I breathed a sigh of
relief. It was Tim, an off-duty patrolman who
worked as a guard at the ice cream company.

Tim held up his hand. "Look, I'm a cop and I
saw it all. This guy wasn't doing nothin'. Those kids
were setting the dog on fire." Silence filled the air.

The people in the crowd stared at me, looked at their kids and disgustedly left.

Tim turned to me, "I remember you. You're a friend of Ellis, right?"

I said, "Yes."

"You look like you're in a little bit of a jam," he observed.

"Yeah, you know it," I flushed.

"Well" he said, "Ellis should be here soon. I'm sure he wants to see you."

I grimaced, "I hope so."

I waited around and finally Ellis, a red-haired, ruddy-complexioned man, pulled up in his car. He got out, and said softly, "Joe, what happened to you? Where have you been?"

I tried to keep my voice steady, "Ellis, things are pretty bad. I really need a place to live, and some decent food. I'm not feeling that good."

Ellis nodded. "Look—you got any family?"

I bit my lip and said, "Yeah, I got some family."

Ellis grunted, "Well, you're Italian. And Italians are supposed to take care of their own."

I shook my head, "Well, I just came from them, and they wouldn't give me the right time of day."

He said, "Joe, I'll do anything I can to help you. But I'm afraid I can't let you stay anywhere in the ice cream company. If something happened to you, I could get in a lot of trouble with the Department of Health, because there's food around here."

I said, "I don't want you to get in any trouble Ellis, but you're pretty smart, and right now my brains aren't working too good, maybe you could advise me what to do."

He said, "Well," he paused and scratched his chin, "my daughter used to work for one of those famous philanthropic organizations in the Bronx that are always helping poor people. I got pretty friendly with her supervisor. I'm going to call her up to see if she can help you." I nodded.

"Come into the office with me." I went into the office. Ellis put a chair next to his desk and told me to sit down and relax. Then he pulled his black leather swivel chair out from under his desk, sat down, picked up the phone, and called up a Miss Bell.

He explained who he was, and apparently she remembered him. Then he said, "Look, I got a friend of mine here. He needs a place to stay, and some food, can you help him out?"

I don't know exactly what she replied, but from the conversation I gathered that it was close to five o'clock and she was about ready to go home. Then he got assertive (he was a very good salesman) and said, "I'll give a donation if you can take care of my friend tonight. Okay I'll send him over there in one of my trucks right now. Righto?" They talked a little more, and he hung up the phone. He turned to me, "She is going to wait for you and help you out tonight."

I said, "Are you sure these people are going to help me?"

He said, "You better believe it. I'm going to give

them a donation to make sure they do. Come with me." He wrote out a check, put it in an envelope, walked over to Gus, one of his men who was loading the ice cream trucks, and said, "Take Joe over to Miss Bell's office in the van, you know where it is. And make sure Miss Bell gets this envelope."

Gus nodded, "O.K."

I got into the van with him. Ellis came over to me and said, "Look, Joe, I hope these people help you out. Don't ever feel shy. Come back if you need to. I'll help you in any way I can. But first you have to get cleaned up and find a place to stay."

We drove to the door of a very famous organization. Gus double-parked the van and said, "This is where Miss Bell works." He got out of the van with the envelope in his hand and I followed him in the front door. I could see an office, and directly across from it was a church. I started to walk in that direction.

Gus motioned to me, "Not there, follow me;" I nodded. We walked towards the back of a big room, past a gymnasium, up a flight of stairs. Then we entered Miss Bell's office. There were several desks there, but an intense, attractive-looking woman with high cheek bones and blonde dutch-cut hair was the only one working. She sat talking to a woman who had a little kid on her lap. They were eating sandwiches. I sat down on a chair near the door.

Gus went over. "Are you Miss Bell?" She nodded. "Ellis called you up."

"Yes, he did." She drew out her words in a haughty manner.

He handed her the envelope and said, "I have to leave but this is Joe, we want you to help him."

"Okay" she said. And then turned back to talk to the mother and child. When they left, she called a few people on the phone and talked to them for about half an hour. Finally, she turned to me, "Come over here and sit on the chair next to my desk." I did. She fired three questions at me. "Are you a drug addict? Alcoholic? Convict?"

I shook my head, "No, I'm not any of those."

"Well then, what's your problem?" She said almost accusingly.

I stuttered, "I need a place to live and some food."

As she was talking to me, she opened up the envelope with the check in it—looked at it. And got furious. Her dark eyes flashed with anger as she said, "You know, Ellis made this check out to my organization, and not to me!" and "It's only twenty-five dollars."

I flushed, "I don't know. All I know is I need a place to stay."

She said abruptly, "Look. Go downstairs, to the other office and give them the check. Right now, I'm busy. I've got to go home."

I said, "All the kids downstairs were eating. Could I have some food?"

She said tartly, "Talk to them downstairs!"

Wearily, I walked downstairs and knocked on

the door of the other office. A morose-appearing, slight man in his early thirties appeared, I gave him the check. Then I poured out my story: "I need food and a place to live."

He stared at me and voiced the three magic questions: "Are you a drug addict, alcoholic, or convict?"

"No."

He replied, "Well, look, it's after five o'clock, and you really don't fit any of our programs. There's an alcohol rehabilitation center about three or four blocks from here. Go over there. Tell them that you're an alcoholic. They'll give you treatment and keep you there a few days."

I said, "I don't want to start lying to doctors and get all doped up."

He seemed surprised, "Well, really, we can't help you here."

I asked, "Well, could you give me some food?"

He answered, "No, we really can't. That food is just for the kids."

Getting up from his desk, he showed me to the door. I opened it and walked out into the street. As I stood by the doorway, he mumbled something through the open door about the size of the check. I got the idea it wasn't big enough for them to get involved. He called after me. "Look, after you get out of the alcohol rehabilitation center, come back here. Maybe we can help you find a job. But right now, tonight, we can't do anything."

I begged, "Can't you just let me drink some water, and wash up at the sink?"

He said, "No, no, no, no. That's impossible. No."

He banged the door behind me and locked it. I was back in the street again, wondering whether if Ellis had made the check out to this woman personally, she would have helped me, or just how much money it would have taken for them to get involved.

I had to think, what move could I make now? In the wintertime, it's relatively easy to get into an abandoned building where you can stay because everybody's huddled in their houses to keep warm. But in the summer, to find a breeze, people sit on the stoop in front of their buildings all night long. If they saw me on their block, they would know I did not belong there and would chase me away. I had to forget about trying to get into another building where I could rest. I slept in the street that night.

The next morning I remembered a man in the old neighborhood where I grew up. "Bill Smith," I mouthed his name. "Finally, I've thought of a friend who might help me." Bill owned a combination income tax and travel agency. I went there. I was lucky. Bill, his dark substantial frame bent over his desk, could be seen through the window in his store front office. I sighed; he was by himself, so I wouldn't be bothering him.

I went in. He looked up surprised, narrowed his eyes, and growled, "What do you want?"

I said, "I have no food or money, or anywhere

to live. Could you let me stay in back of the office or the backyard for a while?"

He frowned, "Look, I can't help you."

I said, "Yeah, but you were my neighbor, and I thought my friend, for about twenty years. You can't do nothing for me even though I helped you?" I looked him directly in the eyes.

He averted his eyes and said, "If you want a hamburger, I'll tell them to make you one in the luncheonette across the street. I have an account with them. But that's it. That's all I can do for you. And I am only going to do it once."

I said "Thanks," and he called the luncheonette across the street.

Then he said, "Go over there now, they'll take *good* care of you."

Walking in the store I ordered the burger. The woman who worked there glanced at me distastefully and said, "You can't eat it here, take it in the street to eat."

I nodded. As soon as I got out in the street, I bit into the burger. It tasted like soap. I spit it out.

Then I thought of another friend from my old neighborhood. His tenants had given him the name "Slumlord." I went over to Slumlord's storefront office in a three-story brownstone. I asked, "Hey, how are you doing? Could I talk to you a couple of minutes?"

I grimaced as I saw another disdainful look.

"What are you doing here?" he said.

I said, "I badly need a place to stay. Could you

get me into one of your empty apartments to wash up, and stay a couple of days and get some sleep? I am ready to fall off my feet."

He said, "I got no vacancies."

I sighed, "Come on. With all those buildings you got, you're trying to tell me you got no vacancies? Who are you kidding?"

He said, "Yeah, I ain't got no vacancies. And I can't talk to you now, because I'm busy. If I have time—later, maybe. Sit outside in front of the office."

I said, "It's awfully hot out there, can't I stay in here?"

He replied, "No, sit in front of the office. When I finish my paperwork, if I got time, I'll come out and talk to you."

I said, "Look. You owe me a favor."

He said, "Yeah, I know I owe you a few favors. Wait outside."

I didn't know what else to do. I sat in front of his office on the sidewalk, with my back resting on his building. The sun was harsh and penetrating. Then suddenly, the sky clouded up and it started to rain, hard, heavy torrents. I went into Slumlord's office and said, "It's raining outside."

He said, "So stay in the hallway."

About two hours later he came out of the office and told me, "Wait here." Through the open door I watched him cross the street, an umbrella over his head, to talk to a muscular dark Puerto Rican guy who was sitting in a big step-in van (the kind that's used to deliver bread).

A few minutes later, Slumlord walked back and said, "Look, I made arrangements where you can spend tonight. You can sleep in the back of the van across the street. You'll be out of the rain. That's all I can do for you."

At least it was shelter, for that I was grateful. I clasped his hand, "All right, thank you."

I walked over to the van. The guy who owned it opened up the back doors. In the back of the van were all kinds of drums, boxes, metal, crates. But there was enough room for me to get in, and I did. The owner closed the doors behind me, then locked them. I lay down on the floor, listening to the steady rain beating down on the roof of the van. The sound soothed me and I fell asleep.

Suddenly, I heard the van start up and begin to move. Startled, I jumped up and called to the driver, through the wire gate that separated us, "Where are we going?" Between sips from a can of beer he answered to me in rapid Spanish. I couldn't understand one word.

Then he started singing in Spanish and making sharp turns with the van. Boxes and drums that were not tied down fell. One hit my side, hard. I felt bruised, nauseous. Then a huge drum knocked me off my feet. I fell semi-conscious on the floor. As I lay there another box hit me in the head. A few minutes later, a drum banged me in the face. Blood spurted from my head, hands, and face.

171

Finally, just after dawn, the driver drove to a place around 124th Street, near the East River Drive and the projects. He stopped the van, got out, walked to the rear, opened the doors and came in. Grabbing me by the back of my pants and shirt, he literally dumped me out onto a little grassy area between the street and the East River Drive, in the rain. Then he ordered, "Give me your money."

I said, "I ain't got no money."

Striding over to his open tool box, he grabbed a pipe, walked back over to me and held it menacingly over my head. "Now give me your money." Quickly I emptied my pockets and showed him I had no money. He said, "Don't you got some paper money?"

I shook my head, "No." I showed him all my empty pockets again. Good thing I had put my money in my sock. Otherwise, I would have gotten ripped off right on the spot. He looked at me, said something in Spanish, and left. I lay there on the grass in the rain, too weak to get up.

A little while later a white-haired woman came out of the project and walked past me looking puzzled. Then she disappeared inside. Fifteen minutes later two cops pulled up in a squad car and stopped near me. They got out and walked over to me. One said, "What are you doing here?"

I said, "Nothing. I got no place to go. I just don't know what to do. I'm doing no harm."

The cop said, "What's your name?" I told him. He said, "What's your address?" I said I had none.

He opened up his ticket book, filled out a ticket and gave it to me. I looked at it, and it said "wino."

I asked, "Why are you giving me a ticket? I'm not an alcoholic."

He said, "You just make it your business to show up for this ticket. Now, get out of here."

I said, "I don't know where to go."

He said, "Look, just get out of here. And if you don't show up for this ticket and I see you, I'm going to lock you up."

I took the ticket and put it in my pocket. I struggled to my feet. The cops got in their squad car, looked at me hard, and left. Then the old woman who had first seen me and had been peering at me from a distance, slowly walked over and asked, "Didn't they help you?"

I asked, "What do you mean?"

She answered, "Well, I called them up and told them there was a guy that needed help."

I said "Help? They gave me a ticket." Slowly I stumbled away.

Sick and weak, I didn't have the strength in my arms to brush my hair, which was now almost shoulder length, out of my face. Sooner or later, I knew I'd fall down and not get up again.

Well, I had one more chance left. I decided to go back to my old neighborhood to see a guy I knew, Frank. He had some big bucks, and knew the right people. I trudged there and began looking for him, but he wasn't around. It had stopped raining; so I sat down on the curb near a partially opened fire hydrant. I figured I'd wash up, drink a little water, and wait for Frank to come by later to see his friends in the candy store where he liked to hang out.

As I was sitting there, some Spanish-speaking people started to mill around. Though in the past we were only nodding acquaintances, I recognized them. I had known them a good part of my life. I never had any argument with them, in fact, I couldn't speak Spanish and they spoke little English.

One woman in the crowd was a lesbian whose face was always bruised. I never knew why. I was about to find out. She came over with a five gallon pail and began filling it with water from the fire hydrant. I could almost read her mind and know what she was going to do when the pail was full. But I couldn't move fast enough to stop her, I was too exhausted. I watched as she lifted the pail high in the air and threw the water on me drenching me from head to toe.

Then she put the pail down, raised her hands and clenched them into fists. "I'm not scared of you because you're a man. I'm ready to beat you up." Taking a cue from her, the rest of the people started to curse and throw things at me.

I began to stumble toward the front of a building that belonged to someone I had known slightly in the past, an old Italian man. He and his wife were looking out their window to see what was causing all the noise in the street. They recognized me, and motioned with their hands *wait a moment*. About ten minutes later, their son Bob, an ex-football player, pulled up with his wife. He stopped his Buick in front of the crowd, walked over to them and yelled "Stop that right now!"

Everybody quieted down. Bob came over to me, and bent down, "Joe, my father just called me. He told me to come right over and help you. You look terrible, what are you doing here?"

I said hoarsely, "Trying to get ahold of Frank. I figured with his connections, maybe he could find me a place to live or help me out with some money so I could get some good food. I don't know what I'm going to do—I need help very badly."

"Come with me," he said gently, and led me into one of his father's buildings. I followed Bob into the hallway of a five story walk-up. I was so winded I plunked down on the steps. His father came out, looked at me sympathetically, and motioned to Bob.

Bob turned to me, "I am going outside to talk to my father to see what we can do to help you." I could see them talking through the open hallway door; then the father left and Bob came back. He said, "Tell me the whole story, how did you get in the jam you're in? Did you break the law? Did you fool around with drugs?"

I said, "No, but bad things still happen."

He knew my parents had died and he asked me about the rest of my family. I told him, "Forget about them, I've tried them already. They would not

give me the right time of day. I even tried a lot of
homeless organizations, and got nowhere. I don't fit
into any of their programs because I'm not a drug
addict, or alcoholic, or a convict."

He kept nodding.

As we were talking, two grim-faced cops
walked in. They came right up to me and one said,
"Stand up. We're going to arrest you."

I said, "Arrest me! For what?"

The cop said, "You're creating a disturbance.
And you're trespassing in this building."

I said, "I am not trespassing in this building
and I'm not creating a disturbance. This guy owns
the building and he invited me in."

The cops looked at Bob and said, "Do you own
this building?"

Bob shook his head, "No, my father owns this
building, but yes, I did invite him in, and my father
knows he's here. He's welcome here."

The cop frowned, "Well, he's still creating a disturbance, and I'm going to lock him up."

I said, "Hold on. About thirty people attacked
me, and you're going to lock me up? Aren't there
laws against mob violence? Mobs aren't supposed to
beat people up."

He said, "Well, that isn't the way we got the
story."

I said, "Well, I don't know how you got the
story. But you want to go in front of a judge and tell
him that you arrested me for attacking thirty people? Are you really going to tell the judge that?" I

might have been tired and confused, but I still had half a brain, and they saw that.

They stalled, and motioned to Bob that they wanted to talk to him outside. I could see them talking through the open door. They were telling Bob something and he was nodding, "Yes, yes." Then the cops got in their squad car and left. Bob came over to me and said, "They told me there's a place I could take you to. The Men's Shelter on East Third Street."

I shook my head, "Look, please don't take me to that place. Don't take me no place. I'll get out of here." I tried to get to my feet, and almost fell.

He said, "Joe, please come with me." I followed him to the back of the hallway. Bob opened the door that led to the well-lit basement. We went down the creaky wooden steps. He gave me an old kitchen chair to sit on and said, "I have to go talk to my father. Just stay here and rest. I'll come right back."

I waited in the basement for about three-quarters of an hour. Then Bob and his father came down the steps to the basement. The father looked at me. And Bob said, "Joe, I'm going to take you where you'll be okay."

The father looked down and saw blood oozing from my feet. Tears came to his eyes. He took his own shoes off and gave them to me. Then he reached into his pocket, took out a little change purse, with some money in it and gave it to me. And he wished me well in Italian.

177

We all walked up the basement steps, then out of the building. I asked Bob where we were going, he said, "Never mind, just come with me." Bob's father went back to the building he lived in and Bob and I walked over to his car. Bob's wife was sitting in the front seat. She got out so I could more easily climb in the back. Bob got in and started the car up.

"Where are we going?" I asked wearily.

He said, "We're going to get you some help."

I said, "All right," and watched as we got on the East River Drive. We exited at Houston Street heading towards the Bowery. I knew where he was taking me. I pleaded, "Please, don't take me to the Men's Shelter. Just dump me in the river. Dump me in the garbage. Please. Don't take me to that place."

He said, "Look, they'll help you. They'll give you food and a place to stay."

I said, "Who told you that?"

He said, "The cops."

I shook my head. "Do you think they know what it's like to stay there?" As we got close to the Men's Shelter, Bob gasped. Derelicts lay all over the street. The stench from their bodies and the neighborhood assaulted us.

Bob sighed, "Joe, you're right. I can't take you to that place. I'm going to take you to somewhere that's much better than this."

I managed a smile, "Well, it's going to be hard to find a place that's worse."

He nodded. He drove uptown to a large hospital complex and parked his car in the parking lot, shut off the engine, and said, "Joe, I'm taking you inside."

I protested, "Look, I ain't going to no hospital. I just need food and rest."

"Joe you need more than that. You're sick. You need medical care."

Again, I protested.

Bob said, "Joe, you're going into that hospital whether you like it or not."

As we were arguing, a security guard came over and said, "What's going on?"

Bob said, "Well, I want to take this man into the Emergency Room."

The guard said, "No, no, no. You can't take him here."

Bob said, "What do you mean I can't take him here? This is a hospital, isn't it?"

The guard said, "Yeah, but not for guys like him. You're going to have to take him over to the City part of the complex. That's about three blocks away." Bob tried to start up the car but it wouldn't start. There was something wrong. His battery wasn't charging.

He told the security guard, "Look, my car won't start."

The guard said, "All right. We'll push it over to the side. And you'll have to call someone to come and tow it away."

Bob said, "Okay. After I finish helping my friend." I got out, and while they pushed the car over to the side, I tried to walk up to First Avenue to take the bus.

Bob caught up with me and said, "Joe, please come with me."

I said, "I ain't going."

Bob grabbed me and said, "You are going." I tried to resist but I had absolutely no strength in my arms or anywhere in my body. I crumpled to the ground. He picked me up like a baby and carried me about three blocks into the Emergency Room of the City hospital. I half passed out on a chair, but I could hear Bob talking to a nurse. Then two order-lies put me on a stretcher and covered me with a sheet.

Bob walked over and said, "I'm not double crossing you, Joe, this is the best place for you. You need help, and this place can give it to you. Good luck. I hope to see you around the neighborhood when you're feeling better."

10

A Welfare Case

For a long time I lay on the stretcher. Finally, a perky gamin-faced nurse strolled over to me, gingerly took my blood pressure and temperature, and wheeled me into a treatment room. "A doctor will see you soon," she promised in a sing-song voice.

About one hour later, a short, slight doctor came in, looked at my chart, stroked his bearded chin and said, "Well, I want to give you some tests."

"Doc, before you start doing all kinds of tests, can't you first give me something to eat and a night's sleep—that's what I really need," I asked.

The doctor answered, "This is not a hotel or a country resort. This is an acute care hospital. If you want treatment, we'll give you treatment."

Because of all my allergies, I was afraid he'd give me medicine I might have a reaction to, so I said, "I'm a Christian Scientist and we're not allowed to have any kind of medical treatment."

He cleared his throat impatiently, "I'm not going to argue with you. Either you let us treat you, or you're going to have to leave."

I sighed, "Okay. I'll leave." Gathering my strength I pushed myself off the stretcher and limped out the treatment room toward the door that led to the street about one hundred feet away.

The doctor must have alerted the security guards that I had refused treatment. Two came up behind me, poking me in the back with their nightsticks. I turned to see them. "Better get going fast," the red-haired one with the Irish face prodded me with his stick over and over. They followed me closely until I got to the middle of the hospital parking lot, then they scurried back inside the hospital.

As soon as they left, I sat down on the pavement, totally exhausted. A few minutes passed as I tried to gather my thoughts. Then the red-haired guard reappeared, "You're going to have to get out of here now," he said fingering his nightstick.

"I'm sick and exhausted. Where do you want me to go?"

He said, "I don't care where you go. Just don't stay here."

I tried to struggle to my feet, stumbling and falling to the ground.

The guard smiled and raised a beefy hand brandishing his night stick over me, "Your face is gonna be all puffed up." I heard the crack of the nightstick against my head. Exactly what happened after that I don't know.

I woke up on a chair in a room with white tiles on the walls. Facing me were two male nurses, wearing long black rubber gloves; in front of them was a portable bath tub. One of the nurses said to me, "You are going to have to take a bath. Take off your clothes."

I peeled off my clothes and he put them into a black plastic garbage bag, then tied a knot on the top of it. I asked him, "What are you going to do with them?"

He said, "Burn them."

I said, "But they are the only clothes I got."

He said, "Don't worry, when you need clothes we will give you some."

My weakened body started trembling. I sat back down on the chair and said, "Let me rest a while."

He said, "We can't wait." The two nurses picked me up, tied a leather strap around my chest and plopped me in the big bathtub.

One said, "Keep your eyes and mouth shut, because the disinfectant in the water burns." They held me by the strap to keep my head above water. Next, I must have blacked out.

When I woke up, I was on the stretcher in the Psycho Ward. Of course, I didn't know at the time that I was in Psycho, but I figured it out shortly afterwards. I met a guy I'd known before in a shelter in the Bronx. This guy was a stoned junkie. Now, here I was handcuffed to a stretcher with my hands behind me, and this stoned junkie was walking around free as a bird.

The doctors kept asking him, "How are you feeling?"

He'd say, "Oh, I need a little more dope," and the doctors would give him as much junk as he wanted, like he was getting candy.

I asked him, "What are you doing here?"

He said, "Oh, my blood levels of methadone were a little low. So I attacked a squad car with a garbage can and smashed up the windshield." He didn't have a mark on his body. And I got beat up for passing out in the parking lot! My only crime was being homeless. It didn't seem right.

A fan blew cold air at my back. I was getting chilled. And no treatment. I lay there a couple of hours. A cop was standing close by. Finally, I called him over and said, "Look, I ain't going nowhere. Please take the handcuffs off. They're hurting my wrists, and I can't sleep."

He said, "I don't have the keys."

"Look, I know someone on the job" (that means a cop). Then I told him my cousin's name and precinct. He walked away and made a phone call. One minute later, he came back with the keys he said he didn't have, and opened my handcuffs. I guess I had said the magic phrase, "I know a cop." Then I started getting treatment.

I repeated to the doctors my story about being a Christian Scientist so that they would hold off on drugs and esoteric tests. I related my need for some food and sleep. The doctors said again, "This isn't a resort."

I said, "Yeah, but you can't do any crazy tests or give drugs to a Christian Scientist."

The doctor grimaced, "Yeah, that's why you're in Psycho, buddy. You can tell that story to the psychiatrists."

A little while later, a tall man with glasses came over to me and said, in that imponderable voice psychiatrists affect, "Just what was in your mind and what were you doing in that parking lot?"

I said, "Nothing, just sitting."

He said, "Now that wasn't what the guard said when you were brought in. He said you were acting crazy, and he had to subdue you."

I said, "Well, the guard ain't telling the truth. You can see what poor shape I'm in. I can barely stand up, no less beat up anyone."

The psychiatrist stood rooted, thinking. "We'll talk again soon, maybe together we can work through all this."

Later, another doctor, a young guy with a shock of blond hair who'd barely begun to shave, approached me. "We've decided to admit you. Either to Psycho, or to an open medical ward. If you're a good boy, you can go to the open medical ward."

I said, "Well, I'll be a good boy."

The doctor nodded putting on the serious, studious face he'd probably learned a year before at medical school, "Okay, then you can go to the medical ward."

"Thanks, kid," I said.

They wheeled my stretcher right to a room with four beds. But the beds were all occupied. They placed the stretcher in the aisle and left me there. Without turning my head, I asked the guy in the next bed, "When is some food coming?" He did not answer. I asked him again loudly, "Hey, buddy, do you know how soon they are going to bring food?" There was still no reply. I raised myself off the stretcher and looked closely at him. His face was covered up with a sheet.

A nurse came in and said, "That's going to be your bed as soon as the corpse is picked up by the morgue."

I said, "You ain't gonna put me in no dead man's bed." I began ringing all kinds of buzzers, making lots of noise. Finally, the young blond doctor came in the room.

He asked, "Well, what's going on?"

I said, "Look, you ain't gonna put me in no dead man's bed. You think I want to catch some kind of disease, and die? Get me out of this crazy place."

He said, "We can't throw beds out every time a

patient dies. Don't worry, we're going to sterilize it."

I said, "Doc, I don't care what you're gonna do, but you ain't going to put me in that bed, period! Let me out of this dump!" I screamed and began to climb off the stretcher.

"Orderlies," my doctor yelled. Two rushed over and held me as the nurses tied me down. "Nurse," my doctor said in a theatrical tone, "send for the psychiatrist."

They wheeled me out of the room into the hallway. The orderlies stood guard over me, waiting for the psychiatrist to come. My doctor, his face flushed, came over to me and said, "You're being very difficult."

I said, "I'm being difficult? You're being difficult, and by the way, Doc, that guy that just croaked, was he one of your patients?" He turned even redder.

"It so happens he was."

I said, "Look, I want a new doctor. Or out of this hospital. I don't want no bullshit, no stories."

He said, "If you keep on acting this way, I'm going to have to sedate you."

I said, "You ain't sedating nobody!"

Then the psychiatrist I'd met several hours before showed up and started talking to the doctor. They retreated to a corner; so I could not hear what they were talking about. Afterwards, the psychiatrist walked over to me, adjusted his glasses, and he said, "Well, what seems to be the problem? You seem to be acting out some serious hostility with all that yelling and screaming and cursing. We are trying to help you."

I didn't even try to make sense of his words, "Look, who wants to go to sleep in a dead man's bed! If you try that, I'm gonna take off. I may be a little crazy, but I ain't all that crazy."

"What do you mean?" he said his eyes widening, "sleep in a dead man's bed?"

I told him how I'd been wheeled into the room with the corpse.

"Ah," he said, looking hard at me. "Aha." Then he went back and started talking again to my doctor.

Well, I don't know what they were talking about. Maybe the shrink told the doctor that he was going to give me a psychiatric evaluation and admit me to Psycho. Anyway, they decided that they were going to put me into another room and a different bed.

However, after that, they never quite trusted that I wasn't going to walk right out of the hospital one day. So they put a guard in my room, and fastened the IV in my neck with sutures and something which looked like a safety pin that I could not pull out. I was like a dog on a leash.

One day led to another. Then my doctor started talking to me about "the way out tests," hospitals always put you through. You name it, they run the gamut. The doctor said, "We'll start you on a battery of tests soon."

I took a deep breath, "I'm responding to the treatment you're giving me now. The food and vitamins are making me feel better. Why press my luck and give me a CAT scan and IVP X-rays that use dye? (That is a form of iodine, which is also found in fish.) I'm allergic to fish, which means I could be allergic to the contrast media and drop dead."

The doctor said, "I am a doctor, not you. And I am willing to take that risk."

I said, "Good, then you take the test."

His face turned beet red, "We know how to treat allergic reactions."

I said, "Look, it's my life. If there were no danger, I wouldn't have to sign for these tests. And I won't."

He said, "Okay, then you are refusing treatment. That means you have to leave the hospital."

A few days later, on a Saturday morning, the doctor strode over to me holding a wooden clipboard. On it was attached a form of some kind. He pushed the board towards me, "Sign this."

I said, "Are you out of your mind? I'm not signing nothing you give me."

"I'm not crazy, you are," he said. "Sign this. You're signing yourself out of this hospital."

I said, "I ain't signing nothing, buddy. If you want to discharge me into the gutter in the shape that I'm in, that's your responsibility. If it turns out that I croak in the street, it's gonna come back on your head."

He said, "Buddy, you're gone." He gave me

some clothes and ordered me to dress. I got dressed. Then he said, "Come with me or I'll have the cops come and kick you out."

I said, "Okay. At least wheel me out of here."

He said, "No. Walk." Surprisingly, I was able to.

Now, although creepy doctors can threaten you, hospitals can't just discharge you like that. They know you know they're legally liable. So, if you're homeless, they discharge you into the social worker's office. It was located right near the Emergency Room. Jim Ryan, the ruddy-faced, booming-voiced, social worker, was a sympathetic guy, "How can I help you? You have to leave the hospital, but I don't want you to be put out on the streets."

I said, "Look, my cousin Bill up in Suffern County said he would help me when I got cleaned up. Before, when I saw him, he was scared to take me in his home because I was sick and might have some kind of contagious disease. You've got to explain to him that I'm clean, and have no diseases."

He said, "Well, the doctor wants you to go to a shelter on East Third Street. He even gave me five bucks to get you there. He must like you!"

I frowned, "Good. Let him go there. I ain't."

Ryan called up my cousin Bill. Bill told him the family would stand by me one hundred percent, but I couldn't stay there now because his mother, Aunt Arlene, and her sister Grace were on vacation.

"They are the ones who would take care of Joe. And where they are, there is no phone. But I will try to get a message to them. Call me tomorrow, to see if we could make some kind of arrangements to help Joe."

Ryan told Bill I was discharged, and had to leave immediately. Bill said, "Look, I can't do nothing now. Call me tomorrow," and hung up.

The social worker turned to me, "I can make arrangements for you to sit in the waiting room all night. But you won't be able to lie down because if the guard sees you lying down he'll have to kick you out."

I nodded, "It's okay," and he made the arrangements. Then I said, "I am hungry, got any food?"

He said, "Since you're not admitted to the hospital, I can't give you any food. Those are the rules." He paused and smiled, "But I'll go out and get you some food, if you give me the money."

I handed him ten dollars and asked him to get me burgers, french fries and a coke. He left and then came back a few minutes later, gave me the food and then went home for the night.

After I ate, I sat up in the waiting room all night. The next day, as soon as I saw the social worker open his office, I went in. He called my cousin Bill. Bill said, "Well, you're going to have to keep him there at least a week, then call me back. Right now I can't do anything." Then he hung up.

The social worker said he would try to get me into a hotel with which the hospital has an agreement, for a few days. He tried, but couldn't. He said,

"Well, this is Sunday, I can't do anything else. But tomorrow my supervisor is gonna be here. He has a lot more pull in the hospital than I do. Maybe he can do something."

Again, I had to sit up in the waiting room all night. I didn't have much money left; so the social worker just got me french fries. By six a.m. the next morning I couldn't keep my eyes open anymore. I went to the social worker's office. It was open, but nobody was there. I thought I'd found a place where I could lie down and the guards wouldn't see me and kick me out of the hospital.

Just as I sprawled out across three chairs, the supervisor came in. He called me by name, because he knew all about me from the other social worker. "Joe," he said, "I'm gonna have somebody see you from adult walk-in. He is one of the head doctors in the hospital. And, really a nice guy."

That turned out to be true. John Townsend, a tall, friendly fellow with craggy strong features, shook my hand and immediately asked, "Why are they putting you out? You were just admitted a few days ago. You were in real bad shape. I don't know if you can remember me. I admitted you. Let me go get your chart." He took some blood tests, and said, "Go sit in the waiting room and try to relax, I'll call you when I get the results."

Later that day he called me into his office. "Joe, you're being a very bad patient. You refused all these tests and we need the results."

I told him I did not want to drop dead from an

allergic reaction to a test I probably didn't need. I said, "Doc, I'm feeling much better because of the food, rest, and vitamins. Can't we hold up on the tests to see if I continue to improve, and regain my health? Why put me through these tests if I don't really need them?"

He explained, "Joe, you're in a weakened condition, these tests are precautionary to make sure you have no serious underlying disease."

I said, "Doc, those tests could kill me. Can't we wait and see?"

He said, "That's up to your doctor on the ward." He smiled sympathetically, "But you're really too sick to go live on the street. Now I can't put you back into the open medical ward, because, somehow, you managed to antagonize a complete medical team and nursing staff. They wrote down in your chart some of the colorful language you used. They thought you created some words just for them."

I said, "Yeah, I got a little upset. And I might have said a few things I shouldn't have."

He said, "Well, the only thing I can do for you is put you in a IMCU (Intermediate Care Unit). It's a special ward which only takes care of people who are not sick enough to be in an open medical ward, but are not well enough to go outside."

I nodded, "Okay Doc, it sounds good to me."

He nodded, "But I'm going to give you one word of caution before I admit you. Don't antagonize all the doctors and nurses on this ward, because I'll have no control over what they do, and if they discharge you again you're on your own. There is no other ward that I can admit you to."

I smiled weakly at him. "Okay Doc, I'll try to be good."

So I was admitted to the IMCU Ward. It was a much more easy-going ward than the one I had been in. My room looked the same, but the nurses and staff were more friendly and courteous.

Now, it took so long for me to get readmitted to the hospital that it was getting dark. Breakfast, lunch, and dinner had already been served and I was starving. So I asked Gail, one of the orderlies, "Is there any chance of me getting any food?"

She grimaced, "Well, supper already came and went. You missed it."

I said, "Yeah, but I'm starving. Can you get me something to eat?"

Gail smiled reassuringly. "Well, let me look around and see what I can get for you." She came back with some leftover food. It was only a bologna sandwich on stale bread, but I was so hungry that it tasted like a feast.

After I ate, my new doctor came to my room. When I looked up, I was surprised to see an attractive woman with a good figure and long black hair. Maria Chin, the attractive doctor, seemed really nice, even though it was difficult to understand her. She kept smiling and tried to explain with gestures and words how sick I really was, and why I should have all the tests the other doctors wanted me to have.

Unlike the doctors in the open medical ward, the doctors in IMCU ward were mostly foreign-born. Their English wasn't that good, but they were more experienced and seemed to care about their poverty patients. Most of them had practiced in other countries and were trying to get an American medical license. They had to put in a certain amount of time in a city hospital before they qualified.

"You," she spread her hands wide, "have to have some tests."

Again I countered with, "But I'm responding to your treatment, right?"

She paused, "Yes, but . . ." her voice trailed off.

I interjected, "You have to hold off on the tests or I'll leave."

She frowned, and as she started talking again, I began to understand her more clearly. "Okay Joe, but I want to tell you one thing. Your hematocrit is seven. A normal person's hematocrit should be around fifty or sixty. You're dangerously anemic. If you go back out on the streets now you will probably die there." She looked at me with dark sympathetic eyes.

I stayed.

11

City Hospital's Cast of Characters

---

*W*hen I started to feel stronger, I got more curious about my surroundings and walked around the hospital talking to people. A stranger bunch of characters couldn't be found.

One day I passed a patient's room and saw a burly cop standing in front of the door. I asked him, "What's going on?"

He said, "I'm guarding this mutt."

I asked, "What's a mutt?"

He explained to me that a mutt is a homeless man.

I flinched, and then remembered he could not tell by looking at me I was homeless since I was cleaned up by that time.

"Why are you guarding him?" I said, puzzled.

He answered rather mysteriously, "Because my people need advancement."

Later, I found out how the procedure works. When a cop makes an arrest, he has to guard his "collar" until the collar gets an arraignment. If the person he's arresting "somehow" gets beaten up, the arraignment is delayed until the injured person is healed. The cop has to guard him in the emergency room until the injured person gets admitted to the hospital. (In a hospital like this, that could take about seven hours.) Then the cop can volunteer to work overtime by sitting guard in a chair in front of the collar's room. Not only is it comfortable, but the policeman gets to eat free hospital food for a few days.

Apparently it wasn't just this one cop that did things like this. According to the scuttlebutt, a lot of cops do the same thing. When they need extra money and a few days off, they find a bum, beat him up, then bring him to the hospital. They get to work three or four shifts sitting in a chair, falling asleep, guarding somebody that's too sick to get out of bed. During that time they get overtime and can get vacation time afterward. So if they figure it right, and beat up a bum before they have days off scheduled, they can manage to get five days off in a row.

Now the bum can complain, but who's gonna listen to anything he has to say anyway? If he says that a cop beat him up for no reason, just how much luck is he gonna have convincing authorities?

So the cops get some vacation time and even rationalize that they're doing the bums a favor by getting them cleaned up and off the streets for a little while. I'm not saying that every time somebody gets "beat up by resisting arrest," it's police brutality. But what I am saying is that there are a lot of cops who take advantage of the fact that they're wearing a uniform and they can make the law suit themselves.

Talk about wasting government and taxpayers' money: When seven cops guard one bum who is too sick to go anywhere, it doesn't make sense.

Still, for me, the hospital food and staff were beneficial. For the first time in months, I was safe and nourished.

Despite the stable atmosphere though, I had three strange roommates. The guy in the bed right next to me was in some kind of coma. He kept talking for hours on end in a language I thought was Spanish and kept me awake. I asked one of the orderlies who was Spanish, "What's this guy saying?"

He said, "I don't know. It's not Spanish or Cuban. He's stringing words together that don't make any sense. He's just babbling."

In the bed across from this man was a heavy-set black man named Jake. He was paralyzed from the waist down, but he was still the bully of the room because of the huge muscular arms he flexed continually. His strength was due in part to nature and in part to the physical therapy he was getting. I think, when you lose the use of one part of your body, it makes the rest much stronger. He claimed he was an ex-prize fighter and a champion. Well, I didn't know if he was telling the truth about that. I did know that he was a bully and gave orders to everybody: aides, doctors, even to the man who babbled in his sleep.

Now, I really didn't like taking orders from anybody, especially a jerk. So when Jake tried to give me orders, I answered him back, "Look, you mind your own business, and I'll mind mine. You don't bug me and I won't bug you."

Well, that didn't quite set right with him, and one day he wheeled his wheelchair over to my bed like he was gonna pass the time of day. As soon as the chair was next to me, he grabbed me by the waistband of my pajamas and tried to punch me. But my pajamas were tied loosely so I jumped out of them, rolled over and out of my bed, picked up a chair and an IV pole, and fought him like a lion tamer handling a lion in the circus.

I used plenty of caution, because I'd seen him use his wheelchair like a weapon one time when he was arguing with a man who was standing up. He aimed his wheelchair into that guy, hitting him with the metal footrest on the wheelchair just below the knee caps. That knocked the guy off his feet and then Jake grabbed him by the neck with one hand, as he punched him with the other till he was unconscious. Afterward, he went into one of the rooms, found a full urinal, brought it back, and poured the urine on his victim.

I told him that if he didn't bug off and leave me alone, I'd tip him out of his wheelchair and crack his head open. That made him back off.

Jake was not in the hospital because he was paralyzed, but because he was crazy. He was trapped on the third floor of a walkup apartment in the Bronx when the building had caught on fire. Before Jake was rescued by the fire department, his mind snapped. He had now been in a wheelchair for years.

Next to him was Ron, a man I used to call "the war hero." He was in his early seventies. When you first talked to Ron you thought he was rational, but sometimes he lost the knowledge of where he was. Then he would tell anybody who would listen about things that happened forty years ago, but yet he didn't know where he was or what day it was. He had to walk with the aid of two big silver canes that had special braces attached to the back of his forearms. Why he was in the city hospital and not in the veterans hospital, I didn't know.

Harry, another patient, was attracted by Jake's private television. He was a dark-haired slick-looking guy, about twenty-eight years old who claimed he had been in every can there was. Each time he walked in, he boasted, "I am a stick-up man." According to the story he told, Harry was in the hospital under a phony name because the New Jersey cops wanted to talk to him about some stick-ups. He was a drug addict who was being treated for endocarditis.

That's a kind of heart infection drug users get from using dirty needles. To treat people with that disease, the doctors put them on an IV which they inject with antibiotics. Since these patients are ambulatory, the IVs are attached to something like a coat tree on wheels.

A patient from another floor kept coming to see Ron; he was a good-looking guy, about fifty years old. He looked like Johnny Carson; his name happened to be Joe also. He kept asking everybody, "May I please have a cigarette?" even if he was smoking one. If somebody gave him one, he would ask them again, "May I please have a cigarette?" I don't know how many cigarettes he used to grub by the end of each day, but those are the only words I ever heard him say in the four months I was in the hospital.

There also was a diminutive Chinese man, about four-foot-five, weighing about seventy-five pounds, who used to come to my room. He would wave at me in a conspirator's manner then hide under tables, beds, and in closets until the nurses found him.

Walking around, I soon found out that the corridors of this city hospital were filled with drug addicts. That's how I learned how many drug users get endocarditis from using dirty needles. I used to hear the doctors tell them, "In the future, if you're going to shoot up, wash your needles with bleach to avoid infection."

Like the drug users who were often repeaters, Harry—who also came to visit our room—was a professional convict. He really knew how to get along in institutions. He clued me in. However, I soon found that he was not to be trusted, because he was a stool pigeon. Once, when Jake was out for some kind of test, the aides brought in lunch and put Jake's food on the table near his bed. That day we had burgers; it was rare that we got something that tasted so good. I knew the aides would be coming to pick up the trays and that they wouldn't save food for anybody, so I took Jake's tray and put it in my closet to give to him if he wanted something to eat when he came back. If he didn't eat the burgers, I would eat them myself later on.

As I closed my closet door, I saw Harry watching me. A short while later, the aides came in to pick up the trays and scowled, "There's a tray missing." (This wasn't out of the ordinary because a lot of guys would take their trays and eat them in the day room or in somebody else's room.)

"Maybe Jake is eating his food in one of his friend's rooms or in the library," I said to the aide. Harry walked out of the room right after the aides left. A few minutes later a nurse walked in, opened my closet door, and snatched the tray. For a moment I was surprised—no one had ever done this before. Then I realized the professional convict had ratted on me to get in the good graces of the hospital staff. I steered clear of him after this.

I met other characters who were not much better; one was Mike, a heavy-set man built like a gorilla. He was being treated for hepatitis and was a drug addict. He claimed he was a button man for the Mafia. That meant he was a professional killer. I did not believe he was a hit man for the mob because anybody with brains would never admit to being a professional killer. But I think he was telling the truth about being a professional car thief.

Mike said, "Every morning, to get started, I need three bags of dope and one bag of coke."

I asked him, "Don't you get sick from mixing heroin and coke? Why do you do it?"

Mike replied, "I don't get sick, it makes me feel great, and if I didn't mix the drugs I would fall asleep from the dope or be nodding out. And if I just took coke, I would be too hyper and talk too much. The combination is called a speedball. It's the only way to fly."

Although Mike was often flying, he was also

friendly and chatty. Once I asked him how he went about stealing cars. "It must be very difficult, especially today with all the elaborate car alarms," I observed.

He smiled, "No, it's really very simple."

I was intrigued, "Tell me how."

He answered, "Well it's very easy. The first thing I do is go to a stationery store and buy a steel ruler around three feet long. Then I cut a notch in it that will catch the little hook on the back of the lock inside the car door. I slip the steel ruler between the glass and the rubber on the car door, catch the back half of the lock where the lever is, grab it, and the door opens right up."

"Pretty ingenious," I said.

He nodded, "Also, I know a locksmith who loans me a special tool which is just about the same size as the steel ruler, so I can copy the locksmith's special notch. That way I can open up almost any car door."

I felt like a stupid kid. "Gee, I didn't know it was that easy."

He said, "Yeah, it is."

Then I asked, "Well, what do you do after you get in the car? How can you start the car up? They got that steering wheel lock, so you can't move the steering wheel or start the car up without the key. What do you do then?"

He replied, "That's even easier. I use something called a slaphammer."

I said, "What's that?"

He answered, "It's a special tool that body and fender men use to pull out dents on cars. It looks like a spool of thread on a knitting needle, but is much bigger and heavier. One end of the slaphammer has a sheet metal screw, which is attached to a strong steel rod—that's the part that looks like a knitting needle. The other end of the rod is fastened so that the slip portion—a heavy piece of metal that looks like a spool of thread—won't pop off.

"Now if you put a spool of thread on a knitting needle, you can whip the spool up and down with your hand. You use the slaphammer by screwing the part that has the sheet metal screw into the ignition lock. Then you put the slip portion close to the screw, and just whip it up hard with your hand once or twice—until the impact from the heavy slip portion hitting the fastened part of the rod, pops the lock out of the steering wheel. Then you put a screwdriver in the empty hole, start the car right up and drive away. The whole operation takes about five minutes."

I asked, "What do you do if they got burglar alarms?"

He answered, "That's no problem, because before I try to steal a car, I reach underneath it and cut the negative battery cable, so the alarm won't go off, then I open the hood, disconnect the burglar alarm, then reconnect the battery with a jumper cable."

I said, "Well, what about these new special silent alarms, that have pagers like doctors have?

They are very sensitive—if somebody just brushes by the car, the alarm will go off on the pager that the owner of the car has with him."

He said, "That really is no big deal. It's just a little more work. I do the same thing, cut the negative battery cable, but then I also disconnect the radio antenna, because that alarm setup has a transmitter that transmits the signal by the antenna to the pager. So I just disconnect the antenna and reconnect the battery cable. It's that simple.

"I also used to take orders for brand-new (stolen) cars. I was able to match the color and the accessories for my customers."

I asked, "Yeah, well how did you do that?"

He explained, "That's also very easy. All I did was go to a new car dealership's service department. These people park cars that are to be serviced all over the place—on the sidewalks, side streets, etc. And they always put a work order (a bill with the customer's name and address) right under the windshield wiper. Then, they either leave the ignition key in the ignition lock, put it behind the sun visor, or underneath one of the mats.

"I would go over to the car I wanted, write down the customer's name and address, and take the keys. Then a week later, I would go to the customer's home, get in the car and drive away. It was just that easy."

"Yeah," I grimaced, "but don't the new car dealerships know something's wrong when they see the keys aren't there? Don't they call the police or make some kind of investigation?"

He replied, "No, they just think one of the mechanics misplaced the keys, and make a new set of keys in a couple of minutes, using coded numbers that they have on file. They never even tell the customer that the keys are missing, so they aren't alerted."

I shook my head, "Is there any real way an owner of a car can stop it from being stolen?"

He replied, "The only things they can do to protect their car is to hook up additional wires to their burglar alarm system that can't be reached from the bottom of the car. This way, the alarm will go off even if the battery cable is cut. They could also have a good hood lock installed, so the alarm can't be disconnected. Those are the only ways that car owners might be able to protect themselves a little bit. But if I want a car real bad, I can work around those things too."

I guess Mike had to accumulate a lot of expertise, because he needed a lot of money to support his heroin habit.

Next I met a young kid, who looked like a picture of the perfect, clean-cut, all-American boy. He claimed to be eighteen, but really he was twelve; his name was Don. He made his living on the street.

He was a prostitute who worked on the meat rack. This is the area around 42nd Street and Broadway, where male teenage prostitutes hang out to meet their gay clients. Don was in the hospital because he was an adolescent diabetic and had something called an "A Line." This meant that the doctors had cut into one of the arteries, in this case in his arms, and had hooked up a little valve so they could draw a lot of blood samples throughout the day. This way, they could work out his insulin dose without causing him any discomfort.

I heard the doctors tell Don many times not to eat in between meals, because it was difficult to work out his insulin dose. Don never listened to them. He drove the doctors especially crazy, because along with having diabetes, Don was hooked on drugs. He popped Valium and Darvon amongst other drugs, and he constantly asked the doctors for pills.

I tried to talk to Don. "Really, there's no future in you being a teenage prostitute. You should try to do something with your life."

He always answered, "Look, don't worry about me, I know how to live on the street. I got some smarts. I can take care of myself."

In a warped way, this was true. I observed him for about a month. Then he started to get in arguments with the doctors, because they didn't want to give him anymore tranquilizers. Don figured out a scheme. He made believe that he was going crazy, and managed to fool the doctors. They admitted him to Psycho, where he got all the tranquilizers that he wanted.

In another room down the hall was a female prostitute, Gloria. She was a very beautiful black girl, about eighteen years old. She was also a heroin user who was being treated for endocarditis; and, of course, she walked around with an IV walking pole. Many times, she practiced her trade with other patients or visitors right in the day room. She would position a few chairs as barriers so that nobody could see what she was doing, and lie down with one of her customers. All you would see was her IV pole jiggling.

In fact, she was a very enterprising young lady. I once asked her, "Gloria, what are you going to do with all the money you're making?"

She said, "If I can stay here a little longer, I won't have any expenses. Anything I make is all profit. When I get out, I'll have enough money to get myself a real nice apartment."

12

Discharged, With No Place to Go

---

*F*our months later, I was fully ambulatory. Since I was no longer sick enough to be in the hospital, I knew sooner or later I would have to leave. I still had no money nor a place to live; so I decided to talk to the social worker assigned to the ward.

"Miss Nasty" had short, gray-streaked, auburn hair, high cheek bones and a haughty manner. The patients used to call her Miss Nasty because she was nasty and had an attitude problem that was beyond belief. When I approached her for help she said, "I want names, give me a list of names. You have to get out of the hospital soon. This isn't a country club or a hotel. Have you a mother or father?"

I said, "No, they're dead."

She replied, "Well, give me some names."

I paused, "There's only one name that I could possibly give you, that's my cousin Bill. He said a few months ago that if I got cleaned up, he would help me out any way he could. He gave me the family's word they would stand behind me a hundred percent."

She asked, "Well, what's Bill's phone number?"

I wrote it out for her. And she said, "Well, that's way up in Suffern County and we're not allowed to make long distance phone calls."

I said, "Send him a card."

She said, in an intimidating tone, "That's going to take much too long."

I shook my head, "Well, that's all I can give you. You wanted a name, that's the only person who might help me."

She left in a huff. Later, when she came back, she said, "I spoke to your cousin. He said somebody from your family will come down here the day after tomorrow to talk to us and to see if we can make some kind of arrangements for you."

I felt better—at least they were not going to desert me. I waited, looking forward to seeing Bill. Bill never showed up. In his place Jay, my cousin the cop, came. I was disappointed.

"The hospital called Bill. Why didn't he come?

He gave me his word that the family was gonna help me out."

He said, "That's all different now. The family doesn't want any part of you."

I sighed, "Why did you come down here, just to tell me that? Why bother?"

Jay looked annoyed, "Because the family doesn't want you making a nuisance of yourself, calling us for help. The only thing that we're gonna do is help you out with a couple of bucks when you get out of the hospital. But we're only gonna do this one time and that's it. From that point on, we don't even want to know that you exist."

I said, "Look, if I was a drug addict, alcoholic, or stick-up man, I could see you being like that. But I've been a legit guy all my life. I would have helped you; why don't you want to help me? I never did anything bad to the family or was disrespectful. What's the big deal about putting me up for a little while 'til I get back on my feet?"

His lip tightened, "Look, there's no big deal. But that's it. You're on your own."

I said, "How much money are you gonna give me?"

He paused, "Maybe forty or fifty bucks."

I said, "You might as well give it to me now, that way you won't have to come back."

He said, "No, you might spend it."

I said, "Where am I gonna spend it in a hospital?"

He replied, "Look, I haven't got any money on me now. Call me when you get discharged."

I said, "Thank you," as he walked out.

Miss Nasty stormed into my room and said, "I just spoke to your cousin in my office, and he made it clear that your family doesn't want any part of you. You're still going to have to leave the hospital. Give me some more names."

I spoke quietly, "There are no more names. That was the spokesman for the entire family. What do you want me to do?"

She began to curse under her breath, "I am going to call for someone from Social Security to come down here and see if you can get SSI or Social Security."

Jack Smith, the salt and pepper-haired representative from Social Security, had obviously been in the system so long that he no longer saw anyone except as a number.

After asking a few perfunctory questions, he handed me two letters that said I had a pending application for Social Security and SSI. "It will take about a year to process the claims," he said. "You will get no immediate help. Call the number on the letters in about a year to find out if one of your claims was approved."

When I asked him what I was to do in the meantime, he shrugged, "Go on welfare."

Afterwards, Miss Nasty came striding into my room, "Let me see the letters that he gave you."

I showed her the letters and she said, "You have

a pending application for SSI and for Social Security."

I said, "Yeah, the guy told me. They might act on it a year from now."

Miss Nasty looked at me hard and said, "You have to leave the hospital very soon."

I replied, "I know. Could you help find me a room or have Welfare open up my case?"

"Absolutely not," she replied, "You have to do that yourself when you get discharged."

"I don't want to go back to sleeping in the gutter. It almost killed me."

Her eyes narrowed and she muttered, "I am sure you are an expert at sleeping in the gutter."

I gasped, unable to believe that a social worker would say something like that, especially after I asked her for help. Then I said, "I may be an expert at sleeping in the gutter, but you're obviously an expert at standing on the street corner."

Her face turned crimson, and if looks could kill I would be dead. She walked out and slammed the door.

During the next few days, Miss Nasty continued to prod me. My problem of finding somewhere to go grew more critical.

The hospital had a number of outreach programs—people who called themselves brother or sisters, ministers, and volunteers who would come around, visit the homeless, and give them a piece of candy or a can of fruit juice. I made up my mind that the next time one of the members of these groups talked to me, I'd make it my business to get their phone number and address. Maybe they could help me find a room or a job.

When Sister Genevieve and Brother James appeared, I put my plan into effect. After I gave them all the information they requested, I asked for their phone number and address. They would not give me that information and said, "God sent us."

I said, "Alright, give me God's phone number and address."

The Sister answered in a serious voice, "We're not at liberty to do that."

I said, "Why won't you give me your phone number or address? You're helping the homeless, aren't you?"

They replied stoically, "Yes, we are doing God's work."

Then I asked, "How can you do God's work if I can't contact you when I get out of the hospital and need a place to live?" I got nowhere.

I decided to stop thinking about what I was going to do when I got discharged. Maybe if I relaxed and got my mind off it, a new idea would come to me. I went to the day room, plunked myself down in a comfortable chintz armchair located in back of a huge fern plant, and tried to hide from the brain plumbers (psychiatrists) and Miss Nasty.

Unfortunately, almost immediately, Miss Nasty showed up. She marched to my hidden corner, bent her head down and hissed, "Get your letters from

Social Security and meet me in my office right away."

With a hangdog look I followed her. "Why do you need these letters?" I inquired, holding onto them once we were inside her office. "You've seen them a hundred times."

"I told you I want those letters now." She grabbed at them.

I held tight and didn't let go. "Tell me why."

We had a tug of war, which ended when she screamed at me, "You're leaving the hospital, period. Now go back to your room." She pointed her finger and stamped her foot like I was a naughty child being reprimanded.

I wanted to answer her back and tell her that I deserved to be treated with dignity; but I said nothing, just retreated to my room—the room I would soon be kicked out of.

That was in 1980, the Friday before Columbus Day weekend. Miss Nasty would not be back in her office again until the next Tuesday, so I knew I wouldn't have her driving me nuts for several days.

There was a ball game on television that weekend—the playoff between the New York Yankees and the Oakland A's. Another patient invited me into his room, and watching Bill Martin's team drew me into the excitement. I forgot my troubles and renewed my love of the game.

But when the game was over, my problems came back to haunt me. I couldn't sleep and went into the day room. Rain pounded against the window. I walked over and pressed my hand against the glass, remembering how it felt to be homeless, living in the streets with the rain pounding down on you. That was something I did not want to repeat, yet I had no place to go.

"God had spared my life for these months that I was in the hospital," I thought. Was it just to go back to sleeping in the street . . . ? My mind couldn't conceive that. It would be like going back to hell. Tears poured down my face. One of the aides came in. She tried to cheer me, "Maybe you'll be lucky and find a place to live."

I said, "Yeah, maybe a jail, or the cemetery. I ain't really what you call a lucky guy. Although I've gotta say, when I look at some of these people in this ward, the ones that have no legs, arms, eyes, I feel I can't complain. I have both my arms, legs, eyes."

But how long I would stay this lucky I didn't know. It was something to think about. I kept racking my brains, trying to figure out how to get myself out of this mess. Was there any possibility, or some friend I hadn't contacted yet? Just what could I do? Was there any way I could avoid going back out into the street again?

Well, my mind kept on working and working, but I couldn't come up with a solution. I had no place to go, no family or friends that would help me. Eventually, I went back to my room and fell asleep.

The next morning, Sunday, I got up around six, feeling very depressed. I knew my time in the hospital was coming to an end. About 8:00 a.m., breakfast came, and about 10:00 a.m., a nurse came over to me and said, "Get your clothes on, you're leaving the hospital today."

I said, "You're discharging me on a Sunday? Are you crazy? And tomorrow's Columbus Day, a legal holiday."

She said, "Yeah, well your social worker signed all your discharge papers. I saw her giving them to you near her office on Friday."

I said, "No, Miss Nasty wasn't giving me discharge papers, she was giving me back my letters from Social Security and SSI that she wanted to look at."

The nurse frowned, "She said you're supposed to leave today."

I said, "Let me speak to a nursing supervisor."

She said, "Alright," and called the supervisor. He came right away.

As soon as he came over to me, I said, "Look, I got no place to go, and tomorrow's Columbus Day. I can't go to Welfare or anywhere else. Where am I going to go, out in the street?"

He said, "Didn't your social worker make arrangements?"

"No," I said quietly.

He said, "Well, let me look at your chart."

He came back a few minutes later, "According to your chart, she is sending you to your family."

I recoiled, "No, my family isn't going to take me."

He said, "Let me call up your family and see what is going on."

A little while later he came back and said, "There must be a mistake. Your family is not going to help you and nobody's going to discharge you today. We'll discuss this with your social worker when she comes back on Tuesday morning."

I took a deep breath, "Thank you."

Now, Miss Nasty was trying to be clever and have me discharged from the hospital on Sunday. This way she wouldn't be responsible. She could say that the nurses discharged me by mistake. If I had kept quiet and hadn't asked to see a nursing supervisor, I would have been cast out into the gutter with no money or any place to go.

This was just one of the tricks that some social workers used to discharge the homeless right back in the street again. It was against the law, and it was also immoral. But who could the homeless complain to?

I spent the rest of Sunday resting up. I caught another one of the playoff games on television. I talked to people about where I could go, what moves I could make when I got out of the hospital.

Monday was uneventful . . . and then, Tuesday morning, around 9:30 a.m., Miss Nasty came storming into my room. She really was nasty that morning because her little trick hadn't worked—I was still there. She spat out her words, "You're gone today, you're out of here. Put your clothes on and come to my office, now."

I got dressed and slowly walked to her office. She said, "I'm sending you to Welfare." Then she picked up her phone, dialed, and said to me, "I'm calling the Director of a Welfare Center right around the corner from the hospital."

She asked for the Director by name and said, "I'm sending this man over to you. I want you to find him a place to live and open his welfare case immediately." She acted like she was giving orders to the director of the Welfare Center, letting me listen to the conversation. But I knew she wasn't talking to anybody, because when you sit close to somebody on the phone, you can hear another voice on the phone. There was no voice.

She was going on and on, making a big story about how my case was going to be opened that day. She tried to make it sound like the Director was saying, "Yeah, yeah, his case is gonna be opened today." I knew it was all b.s., so I snatched the phone out of her hand and started talking. There was nobody on the line.

I asked, "Who are you trying to kid? What kind of miserable person are you? You weren't talking to anyone. The phone is dead."

She answered, "You disconnected it when you took it out of my hand."

I said, "No, you're full of b.s."

She said, "Nevertheless, you're leaving the hospital today. I've gotten you an appointment with Welfare. Now, either you leave on your own, or I'll have the cops kick you out."

I said, "Kick me out."

She handed me some clothes and called the security guards. They said, "You have to leave the hospital immediately."

I objected, "I can't leave because I don't have my vitamins."

Miss Nasty piped up, "You don't get any vitamins."

As we argued, Doctor Chin passed by and I said, "Doc, look, I'm getting discharged and I'm not getting any vitamins."

She said, "You need vitamins. Wait five minutes."

Then she came back with four big bottles full of vitamins and said, "Joe, you really have to take these. You're still very run down. You must eat from the four food groups, get plenty of rest, and avoid stress."

I gave her a tight-lipped smile, "Okay Doc, thanks."

I stared at Miss Nasty and asked, "Where is my two bucks for carfare?"

She handed it to me as if I were a leper. I dressed and left the hospital with a security guard escort. Walking out, I almost felt like the president being escorted, but I could not help wondering how long it was going to be before either I was back in the hospital or in the morgue.

13

Back on the Street

---

*I*n the parking lot, with my cool two bucks for car-fare, I stood wondering whether Miss Nasty had re-ally talked to Welfare about me and whether I really had an appointment. Deep down in my guts, I knew Miss Nasty was rotten and was quite capable of ly-ing.

I had no place else to go but Welfare, so that's where I went. On the way there, I looked down at the clothes Miss Nasty had given me. The white doc-tor's pants, blue and white sports jacket, yellow shirt with red stripes that didn't fit, blue and white running shoes, made me look like a clown. I grimaced. Dressed like this, I was sure I would leave a lasting impression on anybody with whom I came in contact.

At the Welfare Center, I walked into a big room on the ground floor. It was crowded with people who stood on line at a bunch of assorted windows. I got on line in front of a window with a card reading "Information." While waiting, I listened to assorted complaints being voiced: "I don't know why my case is being closed, or why my workers sent me this kind of letter."

Bored, I turned and looked across the room. There were rows of chairs, all filled with people sitting or lying down across them, sleeping. Many women held babies in their laps. I waited and waited, but the line didn't seem to get shorter. Finally, I gave up my place, walked over to the security guards and asked where the Director's office was.

"It's on the fourth floor," he said, "but nobody is allowed up there unless they work for Welfare."

I said, "Yeah, but I got a special appointment to see the Director."

He shook his head and said, "Look, there are *no* special appointments to see the Director. If you go up there, they're going to close your case."

I sighed, "Alright," and sat down again in the waiting area. As I sat there I thought, "I don't have to worry about my case being closed because it hasn't been opened; I had no case.

I decided to take a chance. I walked upstairs to the fourth floor and saw a sign on a closed office door that said, "Director's Office." To the left of the sign, a painfully-thin, dark-haired woman sat at a desk biting her nails. I told her my name and that I had a special appointment to see the Director; made for me by Miss Nasty (of course, I called her by her real name), the social worker at the hospital.

The secretary rolled her eyes and said, "There are *no* special appointments to see the Director. If you have problems, call your worker."

I replied, "I have no worker because I'm not on welfare." I stopped to catch my breath, "I just got out of the hospital, and I got nowhere to live."

We argued for about ten minutes about what I should do. Then a dowdy-looking, gray-haired woman—about fifty-five years old—came out of the Director's office. She looked at me and asked, "What's your problem?"

I answered, "The social worker at the hospital said that she made a special appointment with you to see me, so you could get my case opened up and find me somewhere to live today."

She scratched her head, "Well I know that social worker, but I haven't spoken to her in about eight or nine months."

I replied, "Are you sure Miss Nasty didn't call you, because she *said* she did."

The Director answered, "I'm not responsible for what that lady said. All I can tell you is this, if you want your case opened today, go downstairs to

Applications. If you've got everything in order, your case will more than likely be opened today. In any case, do not come back up here a second time. If you do, I will have the security guards bodily put you out of this building."

I nodded, "Okay." I trudged downstairs and found the place she told me to go to. I got on line again. When my turn came, I was given a form to fill out. Slowly, I wrote down the usual information; Name, social security number, birth date, walked over to a desk and put the form in a basket marked "Application Forms." Then I sat back down and started the waiting process all over again.

Over an hour later a beleaguered young man, whose fingers kept pushing back an unruly cowlick, called me over. I told him, "I just got out of the hospital. I have no money, nor a place to live." He sighed, "You've had a tough time, but do you have any family?"

I answered, "Yes, but they will not give me any help."

He paused for a moment as if assessing me, then he said, "Okay, got any I.D.?"

I replied, "The only things I have are letters from Social Security, saying that I have a pending application for SSI and Social Security. Also I have a letter from the hospital, saying that I was there for a few months because I was very sick."

He nodded, "Well, let me see it all." He read them and smiled sympathetically, "Oh, you were undomiciled when you entered the hospital."

226

I frowned. What a word, "undomiciled"—only
bureaucrats could think up such terms. I nodded.

He said, "Well, we have to find you something."

"I hope so," I answered.

He motioned to me, "Come with me."

I followed him up two flights of stairs to the
third floor. Then he said, "Wait here 'til I come
back." About five minutes later he returned and
pointed to the left, "Someone's going to call you
from over in that section of desks. They'll open your
welfare case and try to find you a place to live today." He shook my hand and said, "Good luck."

"Thank you very much," I murmured.

I waited fifteen, twenty minutes, then a prickly-
looking, red-haired social worker called my name. I
walked over to her desk and sat down on a chair
across from her. Quickly, she scanned my letters
and application, and asked me, "Don't you have any
family or friends, who could put you up for tonight?"

I said, "No, I am on my own."

She rushed on, "Okay, I'll have to fill out some
papers." She sighed and picked up the phone.
About a half hour later, she said, "All right, you're
on welfare; you're going to be getting an emergency
check today for one hundred and thirty dollars and
five cents. Come back here to see me in two weeks.
At that time, you will have to show me a copy of
your birth certificate, social security card, and rent
receipts. If you fail to bring me back any one of

those things, I'll close your case; so make sure that you have all those papers."

"Don't worry, I'll have them."

She nodded, "Take these." She slapped the forms in my hand. "Give them to the people at Housing on the second floor, they'll find you a place to sleep for tonight."

I sighed, "Okay."

When I got to the appropriate place, I put all the papers she had given me on a desk, inside a basket with a sign that said, "Housing Applications." Again, I played the waiting game. This time, I sat in an area in front of rows of desks.

About an hour later, two men, one tall and one short—both bald—who were sitting partnership style at one desk, motioned for me to come over. The short one asked me, "Any drugs, alcohol?"

Tired and impatient by then, I answered flippantly, "Why, are you offering me any?"

Without a smile he said, "No, no, no, I just want to know if you're a drug addict or alcoholic."

I replied sighing, "No, I'm not."

He said, "Well, then we really don't have any live-in programs for your situation. And there's only one place that I can think of that may be able to rent you a room for the shelter allotment in your Welfare grant." The tall one gave me a Bronx address, which I knew was right in the middle of an area in the Bronx that was nicknamed "Fort Apache" by the police.

I grimaced, "That's a pretty rough neighbor-hood, do you have anything else?"

He said, "No, that's it. Just go over there and see if they'll rent you a room."

I replied, "Alright, got their phone number?"

The short one said, "Look, you can't get rooms over the phone. You have to go up there in person and do some talking. Now, to get your check, go downstairs to the main floor and wait for your name to be called."

"How long will it be?" I said dejectedly.

"A few hours, more or less," he murmured, and waved me on.

I sat down on a slatted hardwood chair in a crowded, airless waiting area. Some other guys sit-ting there were dressed just like me, in hospital clothes with their hospital I.D. bands still on their wrists.

While I was waiting, I tried to call my cousin, "the cop." But I had no luck in reaching him.

Suddenly, I heard my name called over the PA system, "Joe Homeless, go to Window 5."

There, I showed my identification to an afro-haired man standing behind the window. He looked through the assortment of welfare checks he held and, finding the one with my name, he passed a re-ceipt through a hole in the bottom of the window. "Sign it," he said. I did as instructed and passed the receipt back to him. Then he handed me my check.

My check. I clutched it in my hand and looked at the amount, "One hundred-thirty dollars and five cents," My heart fluttered; it was small, but for me enough—enough perhaps for a cheap, clean room. Enough to begin my life again.

It was getting late and I was feeling weak and very tired. I went to a nearby subway station and sat down in a warm spot to catch my breath. Without meaning to, I fell asleep. I was awakened, hours later by a tiny white-haired woman asking, "What are you doing here?"

I apologized, "I just got out of the hospital, I felt so exhausted that I sat down to relax for a few minutes and must have fallen asleep."

"Well you can't sleep here," she said.

"I know," I answered, "there is even a song about it; 'Don't sleep in the subway, darling' by Petula Clark. Would you like me to sing it for you?"

She smiled a toothless smile and gave me some religious literature. "You got any place for me to live?" I asked.

"No." She answered, "But pray, maybe then you will find everything in life you want." Slowly, she walked away from me.

I went over to the token booth, bought some tokens, and asked the clerk how I could get to the address Welfare gave me. He peered at me and said, "Aha, Fort Apache." I nodded, he told me how to get there, and waved me on.

The subway soon turned into an elevated train. Looking out the train window as we pulled into the Bronx, I saw burned-out and scarred buildings that looked more like Berlin after an allied bombing raid in World War II, than a suburb of New York. When the train got to the stop near Fort Apache, I got off. As I left the train station, I felt pretty nervous about going into that neighborhood, and wondered what would happen to me if I wasn't lucky enough to find a room.

I needed a pack of cigarettes, so I went to a bodega. As I walked into the store I looked around, surprised. There was only a very small area to stand in. The clerks and all their merchandise were insulated behind bullet-proof plastic partitions. The grocery stores were not self-service. I had to ask the clerk for what I wanted. "Chesterfields," I said.

"Put the money for them through a hole in the bullet-proof glass," he half shouted.

Then I told him the address I wanted to go to. He looked at me, started to smile, and did a little dance, like an Indian doing a war dance, "You know this is Fort Apache?"

I nodded, "Yeah, I know."

Then he said, "Well, around here, that hotel is called Little Big Horn. Do you know what happened there?"

I nodded my head, "Yeah. That's where Custer and his whole command got wiped out to the last man." I didn't know if that guy was joking or not, but it made me think that the hotel that Welfare was putting me up at was even worse than the neighborhood it was in.

As I got closer to the hotel, though, I felt better. It was a clean brick building that was inter-con-

nected to a bar at the corner of the block. In the
lobby of the hotel, there were signs all over the
place that said, "No Loitering." "This is not a Hangout." The signs did little good—there were people
hanging out and loitering all over the place.

Walking over to the desk, I asked the room
clerk if I could talk to the boss. He called him from
the office behind him. When the boss came over to
me, I asked him for a weekly room. He said, "Well,
what do you want in the room?"

I scratched my head, "I'd like to get a bed,
light, and not too many roaches or rats."

"What can you pay?" he asked.

I replied, "Forty dollars a week. I'm on Welfare.
They told me to come to your hotel."

He replied, "Sometimes I have rooms for forty
dollars a week, but not right now. The only rooms I
got available are fully equipped for ninety dollars a
week."

I said, "What do you mean, fully equipped?"

He said, "Well, they got a bed, dresser, and television."

I pleaded, "I don't care about the television, all
I'm interested in is the bed, and a door I can lock
behind me. Can't you take out the television?"

He shook his head. "No, these rooms are quite
a bit larger than the cheaper ones, plus they also got
windows."

I said, "You mean the cheap rooms don't have
windows?"

He said, "Well, some of them do, but the windows are facing walls or alleyways. Now don't give up, people check out of here every day. Keep passing by, maybe I'll have something for you in a few days or a week. But now, I got nothing that you can afford."

I said, "I need a place to live now, is there any place you can recommend?"

He answered, "Not for forty dollars a week. You might find somebody that may let you move in with them, in an apartment. But a hotel, for that money, forget it!"

I replied, "Okay, I'll keep checking with you." Then I left the hotel, thinking maybe it was God's will that I did not find a room in this neighborhood.

14

Riding the Trains to Nowhere

I went to the train station and stood in front of the big map on the wall that shows the whole subway system, wondering where I should go. I had a little less than one hundred and fifty bucks in my pocket. I was not broke, but I felt like a lost soul.

Chills ran up and down my spine, as I thought about where I might be in a few weeks, or in a month—maybe lying in some alley, or back in the hospital, or in my grave. If I could only find a place to live for a few days, with a phone that I could use, maybe I could begin to pull my life together.

I walked over to the phone booth, picked up a directory, and looked up hotels and rooming houses. There were a slew of them. One by one, I called each one, asking what their rents were. I could not find a room for less than forty dollars per night. Twenty dollars worth of phone calls later, I still could not find a place to live. I was just twenty dollars poorer. It was a completely wasted effort.

My mind in shambles, I stood there for a while. Then one of the guards came over, "Hey. What are you doing here?"

I replied, "Trying to think of what phone calls I should make next."

He said, "Look, make whatever phone calls you have to, then leave. This isn't a hangout."

I answered, "You mean I can't stand here and think? This is a public building, isn't it?"

He said, "Yeah, but it isn't a hangout. Now I'm going to ask you again nicely; make your calls and leave."

I made one final phone call, to my cousin, Jay the cop. He wasn't home, and no one in his household was quite sure when he would be.

I started to leave without a place to go. Outside, I leaned against one of the cars, looking up at the sky wondering what my fate was going to be, thinking, "Where can I go?" Then I remembered a hotel on the East side around Eighty-sixth Street. One of my friends used to go there with his girlfriend. He always said it was really cheap, and in a good neighborhood too.

It was close by, so I went there. I asked the room clerk for a weekly room. He replied, "We don't have weekly rooms, only daily ones. They are eighteen dollars a day."

I said, "Can you do any better than that?"

He held up his hands, "Look, I'm only the clerk. You can talk to the boss when he comes around early in the morning. But all I can do now is give you a room for eighteen bucks per night. You have to be out by 12:00 p.m. the next day."

I said, "Well, alright," and paid him.

Then he said, "You also have to give me a dollar deposit for the key in case you don't give it back to me."

I said, "Okay," and gave him the additional dollar. "I'll get the buck back when I give you the key tomorrow at checkout time?"

He nodded his head yes.

I went upstairs to see what the room looked like. It really wasn't bad. There was a double bed, a dresser, and a big mirror above it. Also, there was a window facing an alleyway. When I looked out I could see a string of windows that belonged to other rooms in the hotel. Wearily, I sat down on the corner of my bed, thinking about what I should do next. I had already tried calling a whole bunch of hotels and rooming houses with no luck. What was the next logical move I could make? The only thing I could think of was to find an apartment for one hundred dollars a month.

Going out again, I went to a newsstand and

bought some newspapers so I could look in their real estate sections for a cheap apartment. Scanning them back in my room, I could find nothing close to the numbers I could afford. But the ads gave me another idea. A few real estate companies advertised affordable apartments. "That's one thing I haven't tried," I mumbled. I'd go to a real estate office to see if they had any cheap apartments.

I got the phone book. Inside, I found a bunch of real estate offices that were within walking distance of the hotel. I went first to one, then another and asked them what was their cheapest apartment. They came up with numbers like one thousand, fifteen hundred dollars a month. So I said, "What can you do for about one hundred dollars per month?" They looked at me, laughed, then showed me the door.

I kept on walking around, trying to think of how I could get a cheap place to live. "There has to be some way I can find one," I muttered. "I'm just too stupid to think of it. If other people can find cheap rooms, why can't I?"

I walked down to the lobby and called my cousin Jay to see if he knew any cheap hotels, since he had been a cop in midtown Manhattan for many years. I had no luck in reaching him; so I went back to my room. I had a very depressed feeling in my chest because I was unsuccessful in finding a place to live. I just couldn't get that lousy feeling to leave.

I opened the window looking out on the alleyway and lay down, shutting the lights off to get some sleep. "Tomorrow morning," I murmured, "I'll get an early start on trying to find a place to live. Maybe some idea will come to me."

As the evening settled in, the hotel started filling up with men and women going into a room for a night, their voices—saying romantic things—floated down the alleyway, punctuated by a few moans and groans of joy. In the late night hours, I could hear some of the prostitutes walking up and down the hallways, explaining what cost extra, making all kinds of financial deals with their clients. I listened for a while, then went to sleep.

I woke up early the next morning and washed, staring at myself in the mirror as I combed my hair. Pulling on my clothes, I wondered what the room clerks in the hotels thought when they saw me.

On my way out, I tried once more to phone my cousin. This time I reached him, and he asked if I wanted him to come to see me. Gratefully, I said I did, and we made a date. Then I called up Welfare to ask Housing if they found any new cheap place to live since the last time I talked to them. The guy at Housing said, "I told you the only place I know of. Make it your business to get in there. Do what you got to do!"

I asked, "What do you mean, do what I got to do?"

He whispered, "You might have to give a little money under the table; you know, use your brains."

I said, "All right."

I took a subway back to Fort Apache. Even

though I had a lot of misgivings, I couldn't be choosey. Close to the hotel, policemen had gathered, wearing flak jackets with some kind of helmets. They were being followed by a squad car in the street. It reminded me of one of the old war movies, where the infantry is being followed by a tank.

Inside the hotel, the manager I had met before was standing behind the desk. I walked over to him and began to plead. He kept shaking his head no, but I wouldn't take no for an answer. I followed him to his office, talking a blue streak.

He sat at a desk with a magazine turned face down in front of him. The handle of a gun stuck out from under it. Close to him on the floor, a baseball bat rested on the wall—near it was a bonsai sword. I gulped: obviously he wanted to make sure that he would not be the loser in any kind of an argument. But yet, he made no hostile moves toward me—he was being reasonable. As I was. I even offered to give him a little extra.

He responded, "Well, the bribe would be nice, but I still have no rooms that you could afford. Just keep checking with me; when a cheap room pops up, you can have it. There's nothing I can do just now. Come back maybe the end of the week, or on Monday. A lot of people check out then. That may be your best bet."

I said, "Okay," and left.

As I walked the street, I tried to find a building

that was partially burned down where I could live for a few days. Nothing turned up.

I rode the train back to Manhattan, then got off near a slum neighborhood that I knew about, thinking that I could find a cheap place to live there. I walked around knocking on doors asking supers what was the cheapest apartment they had available. I walked and I walked. I talked and I talked. All that I accomplished was a sore throat and aching feet.

Hungry, I got some food in a deli, and when I paid for it, I realized how much money I had spent for phone calls and carfare. Whatever little money I had was going fast. I couldn't afford to spend too many more nights in the hotel at eighteen bucks a night.

I went to a subway station and sat on a bench eating, looking at people hurrying to get on the train. Everyone but me had a place to go. After I ate, I got on one of the trains and just started to ride. I didn't care where that train was going, because I had no destination. I was just trying to stay warm. When the conductor would say "last stop," I'd get off and get on a train that was going in the opposite direction.

Finally, I got tired of doing that and got off the train, hoping to find a warm spot in a subway station where I could lie down and go to sleep.

I spent that first week and a half out of the hospital sleeping at night on trains and in stations, looking for places to live during the day. I spent most of the money I had gotten from Welfare on carfare and on phone calls.

I was becoming physically and mentally exhausted. I thought, "Before I get real sick, I better spend a couple of bucks and sleep in a bed." I went back to the hotel on 86th Street and got a room.

The next morning when I woke up, I realized I had forgotten all about Welfare. My worker wanted to see my birth certificate, social security card, and rent receipts or she would close my case. I had long since lost all my important papers. Since it was early in the morning, I decided to get a copy of my social security card and birth certificate first.

I went to a Social Security office and told a woman there that I needed a copy of my social security card for Welfare to keep my case open. I showed her the letters I was given by the Social Security field man when I was in the hospital. The woman at the Social Security office said okay and gave me a copy.

I left that office and went down to the Board of Health on Worth Street in Manhattan. I stood in line at the window with a sign that said, "Copies of Birth Certificates." I told the mousey-looking woman with a soft voice, who sat behind the window, that I was born in New York and needed a copy of my birth certificate for Welfare. She said, "It takes about two weeks to get one. You pay $3.00 in advance and then we send it to you."

I replied, "I got the money, but there's no place you could send it to because I got no address."

The clerk said, "Well, you better wait and speak to my supervisor."

The supervisor walked over and I told her why I needed a copy of my birth certificate right away.

She said, "I'll try my best." Although it took almost three hours, I got it.

Then I remembered about the appointment I had with my policeman cousin. I hoped I wouldn't miss him, because I didn't know how long it would take to contact him again.

As luck would have it, the subway trains had broken down. There were people walking out of the subway station, looking for other ways to get where they needed to go. I thought to myself, "Boy, what luck." I found a bus that would take me almost to the door of the hotel, but it was tied up in the heavy traffic for about forty-five minutes. However, I did manage to get to the hotel around 6:30. Wondering if I had missed my cousin, I asked the room clerk if anyone was looking for me. He said, "No." Then he asked me if I wanted a room.

I said, "Yes." I knew I could not stay in the lobby of the hotel unless I had one. I did not want to miss my cousin. After I paid for it, I was completely broke. If my cousin let me down now, I'd be out of luck.

I left instructions with the clerk that I was expecting my cousin to come and asked him to show Jay right up to my room. Around 8:30 p.m., my cousin knocked on my door and called me by name. I opened the door and he came in and sat down.

Then he asked, "How have you been?" and started making all kinds of small talk. I waited, wondering if he was finally going to help me. Then he says, "You know, I was in such a hurry to get out of the house, I forgot to bring the money with me to give you."

I gasped, "Are you joking? The only reason you came down here was to give me money and you didn't remember to bring it?"

He said, "Yeah, I forgot, I had a lot of things on my mind but I'll come down here tomorrow morning before I go to work and give you the money. But after I give it to you, don't ever call me again because I don't even want to know that you're alive, or that you exist. You're on your own."

It was too late, I had been through too much for his words to hurt me. My only goal now was to survive. I said, "Check out time is noon."

He said, "Don't worry. I'll be here long before that."

I nodded, "Alright."

Then he stood up, opened the door and said to me, "I'll see you tomorrow morning." He closed the door behind him.

I went to sleep hungry that night, and got up the next morning around daybreak to wait for him. I started to hear people walking in and out of their rooms, then down the staircase. I went downstairs to tell the daytime room clerk, "If anybody comes to look for me, make sure that you show them right up to my room. It's very important."

The room clerk said, "Okay, don't worry."

I went back to my room and waited. Then, all of a sudden I heard the manager's familiar knock at the door to tell me that it was ten minutes to twelve. I had to be out of the room at 12:00 sharp. I asked him, "Was anybody looking for me?"

He said, "No." I went downstairs to the pay phone, and called my cousin collect to find out what was going on. He wasn't at home, but his wife was and I asked what had happened.

She said, "He was there early this morning but the room clerk said that you had checked out. Try calling him in a few days, because after work today, he is going out of town for three or four days."

I knew it was an excuse, but there was nothing more to say. I hung up.

15

S.R.O.

---

*M*y appointment at Welfare was only a few days away, near but far. I had to live an extra couple of days with no money for food or shelter. I thought if I could make it 'til I got my check, I would be okay, but I was not feeling strong enough to go three days without food and sleeping in the street. I knew that I could not make enough money to buy food and pay the rent in the hotel by begging. I started to rack my brain, thinking of ways I could come up with enough money 'til I got my next check. The only thing I could think of was to go see a few acquaintances who I felt might help me out. I managed to come up with enough money to stay in the hotel a few more days, and to buy food.

When I saw my worker, she said, "Your birth certificate and social security card are okay, but you can't keep on staying in that hotel for eighteen dollars a day. You have to go back to Housing, so they can find you a place to live that you can afford. I'll notify you by mail."

I said, "How are you gonna' notify me by mail if I have no address?"

She answered, "Well, because I'll tell Housing again to get you a place to live. You just make sure that you do what they tell you."

As always, I said, "Alright."

I went back to Housing. Mutt and Jeff were at their usual desks. One said, "Well, didn't you get a room in the hotel I sent you to?"

I answered, "No, I been there a couple of times but they do not have any rooms for $40.00 a week right now."

He replied, "Look, stop playing around. Make it your business to get in there—do whatever you gotta do. I'm putting you in the computer for that hotel. That's where all your mail will be going."

I couldn't argue, I had nothing to say. He had said it all. "Make it your business to get into Fort Apache." I went there, but it was the same story I'd heard before; there were no rooms for $40.00 per week.

I went back to the hotel on 86th Street, got a

room for the night, went out, bought some food, took it back to my room, ate and tried to figure out what to do next. I couldn't think of a thing I hadn't done to find a place to live; I couldn't think of one new idea of how I could find one.

I went to sleep and dreamed of my dog C.T. The next morning when I woke up, I said to myself, "One way or the other, I'm gonna get a place to live today." As soon as I walked out the door of the hotel I saw a beautiful black girl standing in front of the building. Her shapely body revealed by a white silk dress, she looked at me and smiled. Then she asked, "Do you want some pleasure?"

I replied, "Yeah, but I ain't got no money and I don't think you're looking for a boyfriend, especially one with my problems, right?"

She laughed, "What's your problem?"

I answered, "I'm on Welfare and I can't find a place to live with the few bucks they give me. I don't know what to do. I have been looking for weeks with no luck."

She replied, "That's your only problem?"

I said, "Yeah."

She pointed to a building on the corner of the block, "Go in there and ask for Eli. Tell him Lisa recommended you."

I said, "Okay." Quickly, I walked up the street to that building. There was a heavy wood door with no name on it. I pushed on it, it was open. I went inside and climbed up a long flight of wooden steps that led to an office. Then I went in and stood at the counter. A room clerk appeared; I asked for Eli. Eli wasn't there, but when I mentioned the prostitute's name to the man he said, "Oh, you're a friend of Lisa's. What can I do for you?"

I said, "Do you have any weekly rooms for $40.00 per week?"

He said, "No, but I have one for $45.00."

I replied, "Good, I'll take it."

He answered, "Do you want to look at it?"

"Has it got a door with a lock? A bed?"

He said, "Yeah."

I said, "Beautiful, I'll take it." I paid him and he gave me the key and a receipt. I took the key and walked upstairs to the third floor. The room was extremely small. But it had a bed, light, and even a sink. "Perfect," I murmured, "who could want more?" For the first time since I'd been cast out on the streets, I was not a homeless person. I had a place, albeit temporary, to live in and call my own.

16

Landlord and Tenant Court

---

*T*hanksgiving came. Many of the tenants in the hotel complained that the place was creepy and the landlord lousy. To me, it was paradise. I would tell them, "If you ever lived in the streets or spent a night in a shelter, you would be as grateful as I am. You shouldn't call this place a dump."

Since I was going to be living there a while, I explored the hotel. There were over fifty rooms, with two bathrooms on every floor. The people who lived there semi-permanently, like me, were on the third floor. The hotel management wasn't interested in renting their other rooms on a long-term basis. Prostitutes would rent them eight to ten times a night and provide the owners with a fast replenishing income.

The other tenants griped about it, but I didn't care. I had no money; so I couldn't play around. If the girls didn't bother me, I wasn't gonna bother them. In fact, I got to like most of them. They were always cheerful and had plenty of jokes to tell.

In the past, I had thought I was an experienced man who knew all about the birds and bees. But talking to these girls made me realize how much I didn't know. It was really a learning experience. I still remember the way they used to describe some of their exploits with their customers. One prostitute was a man, who would dress up like a woman. His tricks never knew that he was not a she but actually a guy. He was very popular.

The more I walked around the neighborhood, the more I liked it. There were two five-and-ten-cent stores, loads of supermarkets, delicatessens, restaurants, bakeries. Any kind of delicacy and exotic food was available—that is, if you had money, which I didn't. But after living on the street for so long, just to live amidst such plentitude was great.

Christmas was coming. I didn't let anyone dampen my spirits. Since there were few people to talk to except the prostitutes, who were often too busy, I bought a cheap portable radio for companionship. I listened to nutrition experts like Carlton Fredricks, Ronald Hoffman, Robert Atkin and Garry

Nulls. (Their advice has helped keep me alive these many years on the streets), to the ball games and radio talk shows like Patricia McCann, my favorite host.

One day, I heard a reporter talking on the radio about how he went undercover for three days as a homeless man, trying to live on the streets and sleep in subway stations. Later, he wrote of all the hassling he had encountered from the cops and the people in the neighborhoods he was in.

The talk show hosts were shocked at the details he gave, even though nobody had tried to set him on fire, beat him with clubs, or set dogs on him. I thought to myself that all the things he was not telling could fill a book, maybe two. That was when I decided to tell my story.

I knew it wouldn't be easy for many reasons, one of which was I couldn't spell or type. Nevertheless, I was determined to do it.

A few days later I found a broken tape recorder in the trash. I got it to work and began to record my book anytime I could find a place with no people around.

The Christmas season fled. Freezing weather seemed to stay. I was grateful to be off the streets.

Then, in late February, the prostitutes who would hang out in the hallways all night to meet their customers vanished. When I went to the office to ask about them and pay my rent, the old room clerk wasn't there. A short, grey-haired man, pale complexioned man sat behind the desk. "I'm Jake,

the agent for the landlord." I told him I wanted to
pay my rent.

He said, "What room do you live in?" I told
him. Then he stood up and jingled the change in his
pocket. "Look, we want to remodel this place and
have to empty all the rooms first—so move out. Find
another place to live!"

I replied, "Hold on. Here's my rent. I'm paying
it. Give me a rent receipt." He accepted my rent and
gave me the receipt.

Then he said again, "We're gonna remodel this
hotel. We want everybody out. Find another place to
live."

With the prostitutes gone, two-thirds of the hotel was already empty. That just left people like me
in weekly rooms. In a few month's time, there were
only about ten tenants left. And Jake, the agent, was
really getting obnoxious. He said that we had to
move out, regardless of how old the tenants were or
how many years we had been living there. He would
constantly knock on my door at 5 a.m. to wake me
up and ask me, "When are you gonna leave? Have
you found another place to live?"

The next time I paid my rent I told him, "Since
you are an expert real estate man, can't you find me
a place to live at a rent I can afford?"

He said, jingling those ever-present coins, "I'll
try, but you keep looking too." For the next few
months, he gave me a hard time every time I paid
him. Then one month he flatly refused to accept the
money.

He said, "Joe, I will let you live here for free. Save all your rent money, use it to find another place to live. This place is going to be closed up— period."

I couldn't force him to take the rent. (At that time I didn't know that the law was that a landlord must accept the rent if it's paid on time. I found this out too late for it to do any good.) I said, "Alright, I will keep looking for a place to live."

About four months later, the agent came to my room at 5 a.m. to ask me when I was going to move out. "I still haven't found a place to live," I told him.

"If you want to keep living here you'd better give me the thousand dollars you owe me in back rent."

"What thousand dollars?" I asked surprised. "Let me get my receipts." I went upstairs, got them and trudged to his office. "Look here are the receipts. I'll pay you any money I owe you and not a penny more."

About a week later, on a late Friday afternoon, I was served with a Dispossess Summons by the agent and a processor. It said to appear before the clerk in Room 118 at Landlord and Tenant Court within five days.

First thing Monday morning, I went to court and got a court date.

Nervous and apprehensive, I got up early on the day of my hearing, hoping the judge would agree with me. At the head of the stairway right near my room, a huge burly man who worked for the agent stood holding a hammer, smashing in a round knob at the edge of the bannister. He glared at me and blocked the stairway. "Looks like a head doesn't it."

I swallowed hard and tried to appear unafraid. I knew if I didn't make the court date the agent would win a default judgement. So despite the hefty difference in our size and weight, I looked him in the eye and said, "Get out of the way, jerk."

Surprisingly, he stepped aside. I hurried down the stairs and outside, making my way as quickly as I could to the court house.

The room where the hearing was to be held was intimidating. It was about the size of an auditorium. A white-haired, black-robed judge sat in front. Next to him, making announcements, was a short man with glasses, who I guessed was the clerk.

As I walked down the aisle to sit in one of the rows of bench seats, Jake, the agent for the landlord, walked into the room. He looked startled that his trick with the goon hadn't worked and that I had showed up. He walked over to me, jingling the change in his pocket as he always did. As if he was my friend, he sat down next to me on the bench on which I was sitting and whispered, "I have to make a phone call—when they call our names, say 'here and ready'." Then he got up and left the room. Later, I found out that he'd called his lawyer to come down and represent him.

When our names were called, I walked over to the clerk and said, "Here and ready." The clerk gave me the number of the hearing room where my case would be heard.

Afterward, the agent and his lawyer walked over to me. "My lawyer would like to talk to you," Jake said. "Maybe we can work this out."

The balding lawyer had a slight stutter. "I would like to ask for an adjournment," he stumbled over the last word.

"Okay with me," I said, breathing a sigh of relief, thinking my troubles might now be over.

A few weeks later, when we were back in court, I found out the real reason they wanted an adjournment that day was that the lawyer who had been dispatched to represent Jake knew little about these cases. Now Jake had with him an L & T expert, and as soon as he opened his mouth I knew I was out of luck. I pleaded with the judge to appoint a lawyer for me. He looked sympathetic but shook his head.

"I don't have the power to do that," he explained, "this is not a criminal case. L & T court is part of small claims. All I can do is give you some time." He adjourned the court.

Legal Aid was on strike, and I couldn't find anyone willing to defend my case; so I spent the time trying to prepare my own defense. Of course, back in court, the agent's L & T expert out-maneuvered me in minutes.

A few weeks later I was evicted. However, when I went out in the streets this time, I knew from past experience that it was a waste of time to run around looking for help from friends, family, church or charitable groups. If I wanted to survive, I would have to find a way to do it myself.

That day, trying to keep warm, I went to a subway station in midtown Manhattan. A threadbare guy was sitting on the floor near the token booth. As I drew nearer I noticed he had a cup attached to a cardboard sign next to him. The sign read:

I am homeless
Please help

Standing there, I watched person after person drop money into the cup. He was panhandling. At first I felt horrified, then amazed, then decisive. Here was a way to get money for food and keep on working on my book until I could get back on my feet.

17

Becoming a Celebrity

Several years and tape recorders later, I had dictated about thirty-five, sixty-minute cassettes made in basements, burned-out buildings, and on rooftops. They told my story.

I called up several well-known publishers to sell them my book and found out that they do not talk to authors or accept tape recordings as a manuscript. They said I must get a literary agent to sell my book to them, and the only place I could find one was in a book called the *Literary Market Place* which I could get in the public library.

I did as they suggested, made a list of agent names, and called up about twenty that gave me the same answer. My book must be typed, double-spaced, on 8½ by 11 inch paper before they would even think about being my agent.

There was no way I could pay somebody to type my book; so I began to ask people who stopped to give me money as I was panhandling, if they knew how to type and could they do some typing for me. I don't know how many people I asked before a few said okay. However, none of them actually got around to doing it, and then months later, gave me back my tapes and said they did not have the time to do any typing for me.

My efforts went on like that for a year. Then I met Julie one Spring day, in 1985, in the subway station on her way to work. As she stopped to give me a quarter, I asked if she could do some typing for me.

Julie said, "No, I don't have the time, but my girl friend is trying to learn word processing on my computer, maybe she will. Here's my home phone number, call me in a few days and I'll let you know."

When I called her up Julie said her girl friend would not do it, but did ask, "Have you ever thought about making an appeal for typing volunteers on WBAI Radio? There is a show called "Listeners Active for the Homeless" that may do it. The show comes on at eight o'clock in the evening every Friday night, and in the last part of the show they take phone calls on the air. Call them up and ask them to help you."

I said, "It sounds like a good idea, but I don't know if I could find a pay phone that worked exactly as they announced they would start taking phone calls, or if I would have a quarter to make the call."

Julie replied, "Okay, I'll do it for you."

That is how I got the first member of my staff. I was lucky. Julie had experience working for a magazine and book publisher as an editor. She gave me good advice about completing my book and having it published.

After Julie called up the show, the staff of Listeners Active for the Homeless appealed to their audience for five consecutive weeks for typing volunteers. There was only one reply—a girl in her twenties who was working in one of the better known agencies for the homeless. I called her up and made an appointment to meet her at the agency with a few tapes.

I thought I had it made. When I met her, she said, "I'm a law student and I am only going to be working in New York for two weeks more before I go back home to Virginia and my college there. But I'll do as much typing as I can on the agency word processor, because I don't have one where I'm staying. Give me your tapes and call me in a week."

I called her a week later and she said, "I only could do fifteen pages because other people had to use the computer, and I can't do anymore."

I said, "Okay, can I get them and the tapes back?"

She replied, "Yes, come up here now. I am on my lunch hour, so I will have some time to talk with you."

When I met her, she gave me my tapes and the typing she had done. Then she said, "My supervisor was not very happy about my typing your book, and wants to meet you. She is in now—come with me into her office."

She brought me into her supervisor's office and left me. The supervisor asked me, "How many books have you written?"

I answered, "None, I can't even type."

The supervisor replied, "My friend, we are very well known and we can't have our name linked to some screwball. Before we can give you any help, you must have some of your writing published. Then I'll read it and if it is credible, I will give you as much help as the agency can, but not till then."

I asked, "How can I get my writing published if I can't type?"

She answered, "You're a pretty smart guy, figure it out."

I said, "Okay," and left.

Then I called up the member of the Listeners Active group who used to give me my messages and told them to keep putting my appeal for typing on the air, because the girl who had agreed to do typing for me was only able to do fifteen pages.

He said, "It's been on for five weeks, I don't

know if we can keep on doing it, but call up Moogy Klingman, he is a member of our group who said he would like to do some typing for you." He gave me Moogy's phone number.

I called him and we made an appointment to meet in Greenwich Village, near Tompkins Square Park in Lower Manhattan. Moogy and I hit it off as soon as we met. We discussed politics and philosophy among other things.

Then Moogy said, "I did not volunteer to do typing for you before this, because I thought a lot of the other Housing or Homeless Activists would. Also, I thought you were a drug addict or alcoholic. But Lisa, the waitress who I date, said she knows you and you're not an addict, but instead you're into vitamins and health food."

I replied, "That's right—what do you think keeps me alive, living the way I do."

Moogy said, "I am a freelance songwriter; I really don't have much spare time and I don't want to write during any of it. However, the truth about what is going on with the poor people and the homeless has to come out. Before I do any typing, though, you are going to have to give me your word that you won't get disgusted and give up the book."

I told Moogy, "I will finish it or it will finish me. I am going to do everything I can to see the book gets published and the truth comes out."

We shook hands, and in two weeks, despite getting locked up during a demonstration at Tompkins

Square Park on behalf of the homeless, Moogy gave me fifty typed pages.

Julie and Moogy convinced me it was enough to look for a literary agent. I thought it would be easy but, of course, it wasn't. I called about thirty agents before I found one that would even look at my book to see if she would accept me as her client.

I met her in a combination office and home in Lower Manhattan. I handed her my manuscript. She did not even look at it, but instead asked me a lot of questions, obviously trying to get an idea of how my mind worked. Then she said, "Call me in two weeks and I will let you know if I want to handle your book."

A bit discouraged, but not about to give up, I said, "Okay," and left her office.

I telephoned her two weeks later and she said, "Your book is great, but . . ." "But" was a word I knew a lot about. I waited for the other shoe to drop. "It is not written professionally. There are too many grammar mistakes. Before I can show it to a publisher, a good editor has to clean it up. The best thing I can do for you is get a co-author to write your book."

I said, "Look, all that I need is somebody to do the typing, not a ghost writer."

She replied, "If you don't take my advice and accept a co-author, I can't take your book. Moreover, if I get one for you, there will be a charge of fifty percent of all proceeds of your book for the writer, and my fee is fifteen percent. That's the deal, take it or leave it."

I swallowed hard, "I'll leave it." I said to myself, *"Before I go looking for another agent, I will have my manuscript completed so I won't have to hear anymore about a co-author just to do typing and fix up my English. But I'll do whatever it takes to get the book published. If God gives me the brains and health to do it."*

I was committed to getting my manuscript published. I still didn't know how to do it, though. One day, a woman who stopped to give me some change was passing the time of day with me; I told her of the problem I had with my book. She said, "I know a literary agent who attends meetings with me. I will ask her what she thinks. Here is my phone number; call me in a few days. I'll let you know what she says."

When I telephoned her, she said, "The agent wants to talk to you. Here is the phone number, call her up."

I did and told her about the book. "Unfortunately," I said, "the manuscript is somewhat of a mess."

She replied, "Let me see it, then I will tell you what I think you should do."

I brought it right over. "Give me a little time to mull this over," she said.

Although I had hoped for a quick answer, I agreed. Several weeks later she made contact with me. "It is a great story. Maybe I can get a publisher to buy it. I am only going to be in New York City about two more months before I go to Los Angeles to work in a movie studio. Let me see what I can do for you."

Months passed, I heard nothing. Then we had a meeting and she said, "I had a few publishers interested, but they backed off because the manuscript needs a lot of editing and you have also never been published before. You are a real U.F.O. If you had been published or were a celebrity, I think your book would go over big. But not now. Try to retype your book; see what you can do to make yourself famous or get some of your writing in print. If you do all three, you'll have a good shot."

I took her advice. First, I badgered and solicited and created a staff which grew to about thirty volunteers, recruited largely from rush-hour subway platforms. During the next four years, musicians and writers, editors and lawyers transcribed and edited the cassettes on which I had dictated my story

I set about getting some of my work published and becoming a celebrity.

A few weeks after I had gotten this woman's sage advice and spent a great deal of time trying to figure out a way, in my penniless, homeless state, that I could follow it, I read a story on the homeless in the New York *Daily News* magazine. It was filled with generalities that only someone who lived on the streets could correct. I decided to telephone the magazine and was put in touch with its managing editor, Harriet Lyons.

"You missed by a mile," I said when she got on the phone.

Taken back she asked, "How would you know?"

"I'm one of those homeless you're writing about."

She wanted to meet with me. I suggested the only place available to me, a cranny at Grand Central Station where, along with two other reporters, she interviewed me.

When the story ran, one of the people who read it was Toby Axelrod, an assistant reporter for the *The New York Observer* and later a reporter at *Jewish Week Magazine*. She began to help me edit my manuscript and when *Street News*, a publication for and about the homeless came out, Toby said, "I've told them all about you, Joe. They're looking for homeless writers. Call."

Well, I did and that is how I met Eric Berman, *Street News*'s managing editor. He looked at excerpts from my manuscript, liked them, and used one in the paper.

Within a week after *Street News* came out, Katharine—at Richard Curtis's Literary Agency— saw my article and called me.

"The article mentioned Joe's manuscript. I was impressed and asked Richard if we could request it. He agreed. Soon afterward, Joe and Richard met, liked each other and . . . ," Katherine offered.

And finally I had an agent.

My staff of volunteers concentrated on retyping, while Richard and I mulled over what would be best in marketing the manuscript.

About the same time, Eric Berman decided to devote an issue to shelters. Again, I wrote an article. Unfortunately, soon afterward, *Street News* had a variety of problems, including being the target of an investigation. Berman started another newspaper, *Crossroads*, and I wrote its cover story, "Subway Vampires." Despite our enthusiasm, *Crossroads* didn't survive long.

In the meantime, *Newsday* did a story on the homeless. Like the one in the *Daily News*, it too, was filled with generalities. When I called I was put in touch with Mort Persky. After filling him in on what I consider the real truth about the homeless, he asked to see my stuff. I sent it right over.

One year later, I telephoned Mort and asked, "What happened?"

Mort said, "Look, we can't use it all. Pick four or five excerpts and polish them."

I got Toby to edit them and another volunteer, Linda, to type them up. Then I sent the batch back to Mort.

A few days later, Mort announced, "We're using them. Come over and we'll talk."

On October 28, 1990, I, Joe Homeless, became the cover story for the *Newsday Magazine*. Once the article appeared, despite my picture being shrouded in shadows, people began approaching me on the streets and in subway stations, asking if I was Joe Homeless. To my surprise, they asked for autographs.

Patricia McCann was doing a radio show on the homeless. Having achieved minor celebrity-hood, I called her and we did a call-in show together. Then she did a second show. This one was about me; Julie and two of my other volunteers, Moogy Klingman and Linda Sullivan (who had typed 100 pages for me), also appeared.

Julie mentioned my manuscript on the radio. Patricia said she had tried to contact an editor at *The New York Times* about it, but hadn't received a reply.

Out jogging that cold winter night, editor Edwin McDowell, heard that second broadcast and later called Patricia to say, "I'd like to see the manuscript by a homeless man."

After reading it and talking to me, he enthusiastically recommended some agents and publishers.

Over the years, we have stayed in touch and he has given me good council.

More radio shows and print articles followed McCann's show.

So, as far as that agent's sage advice goes, I have done all three things she recommended: had my manuscript edited, got my writing into print, and become a celebrity.

Moreover, I have done them all while trying to survive on the streets of New York.

Afterword

*T*here are no radios or televisions in the street. There are newspapers, but the homeless use them to sit on or cover themselves with in winter. They rarely read them. Also, a homeless person may be a little upset or disoriented after being shoved into a police van or squad car and forced to go, against his will, to a hospital.

The homeless also suffer from malnutrition and dehydration, and often they may have been on their feet for three or four days without sleep.

There are a lot of addicts, alcoholics, and crazies on the street. But bums are not all addicts, alcoholics, and crazies; just some of them, like "normal people" who have homes. Many addicts, alcoholics, and crazies live in houses. But if you live in the street, you are stripped of your humanity, and you do become a talking animal.

When you're in the Army, and in a war, there's something called R&R—rest and relaxation. Entertainers go out and entertain the troops. But nobody goes anywhere to entertain the homeless. It is hell all the time.

But I still don't want to go to a shelter. Most people ask: Why not?

I have never been in a concentration camp. This is the United States, where we have no concentration camps. People say there is a difference. A shelter you can leave, and a concentration camp you cannot. Well, that's almost true. However, when the temperature is below 32°F, the cops force you into a shelter, and you cannot leave.

Since this is a free country, the rest of the time you have a choice. If you don't want to go to a shelter, and you resist, they'll take you to a hospital and bring you into "psycho" for evaluation.

If you wind up in the Psycho ward, they put a rap on you that will stick with you for life—and after it's over, too. The rap is: You're a former mental patient. How many times have you seen a headline about a "former mental patient"? If a homeless man is set on fire or otherwise killed after he's dis-

272

charged from "psycho," you will read about "a former mental patient," not "a human being murdered."

On the streets you're constantly under stress, constantly hungry and thirsty. What kind of a mental state can you possibly be in, even if you were normal when you started? And if you do seem a little disoriented, does that mean that you're crazy or insane?

No one understands what being homeless entails. Nor does the media ask: "Why are there so many homeless people. Why are landlords allowed to warehouse rooms? Why aren't the homeless at least given enough money to buy food?"

Nobody asks those questions, which are mostly about welfare. After all, what do you need to qualify for welfare? All you need is nothing, and the homeless have plenty of that.

I don't have all the answers to the problems of the homeless. But I think that people should know what it's like to be in the streets, the shelters, or the hospitals. If they did, they might be a little bit more compassionate toward those that are. They might know that they actually have our lives in their hands.